The Shippe of Safegarde
(1569)

by Barnabe Googe

Medieval and Renaissance Texts and Studies

Volume 229

A newe Booke called the Shippe of safegarde, wrytten by G. B.

Anno. 1569.

Imprinted at London by W. Seres.

Title page of A *newe Booke called the Shippe of safegarde.*
By kind permission of the Folger Shakespeare Library, Washington, DC.

THE SHIPPE OF SAFEGARDE
(1569)

by Barnabe Googe

edited by

Simon McKeown
&
William E. Sheidley

Arizona Center for Medieval and Renaissance Studies
Tempe, Arizona
2001

Dust jacket image: Emblem 9 from Peter Isselburg, *Emblemata Politica in aula magna Curiae Noribergensis depicta* (Nuremburg: Wolff Endters, 1640). By kind permission of the Librarian, Glasgow University Library.

Library of Congress Cataloging-in-Publication Data

Googe, Barnabe, 1540–1594.
The shippe of safegarde / by Barnabe Googe ; edited by Simon McKeown & William E. Sheidley.
p. cm. (Medieval & Renaissance texts & studies ; v. 229)
Includes bibliographical references and index.
ISBN 0–86698–271–X (alk. paper)
1. Polycarp, Saint, Bishop of Smyrna—Poetry. 2. Allegory. I. Title: Shippe of safegarde (1569). II. Title: Ship of safeguard. III. Eusebius, of Caesarea, Bishop of Caesarea, ca. 260–ca. 340. Ecclesiastical History. IV. McKeown, Simon, 1967– . V. Sheidley, William E. VI. Title. VII. Medieval & Renaissance Texts & Studies (Series) ; v. 229.

PR2279.G4 S48 2001
821'.3—dc21 00–045354

∞
This book is made to last.
It is set in Goudy, smythe-sewn,
and printed on acid-free paper
to library specifications.

Printed in the United States of America

CONTENTS

LIST OF ILLUSTRATIONS

ACKNOWLEDGMENTS

The editors are grateful to the Folger Shakespeare Library in Washington, D.C., for permission to use its copy of *A newe Booke called the Shippe of safegarde* as the basis for the present edition, to the Newberry Library in Chicago and the John Rylands University Library, Manchester, U.K., for access to their copies of the same, as well as to the staffs of those libraries and of the following additional repositories for their assistance: the British Library, London; the Queen's University Library, Belfast; the Warburg Institute, University of London; the Bodleian Library, Oxford; Keele University Library, Staffordshire; the Homer Babbidge Library of the University of Connecticut, Storrs; the University of Southern Colorado Library; the Kraemer Family Library of the University of Colorado, Colorado Springs; the Tutt Library of The Colorado College, Colorado Springs; and the United States Air Force Academy Library, USAF Academy, Colorado.

They also wish to express their sincere thanks to the following mentors, colleagues, and others for their help and encouragement: Dr. Raymond A. Anselment, University of Connecticut, Storrs; Dott. Elena Calogero, University of Florence; the late Mrs. H. L. Chershyn of Don John House, Canterbury; Mr. Roger Davey, East Sussex Records Office, Lewes; Mr. J. Karlin, Lamberhurst Local History Society; Ms. Rosemary Kent, The National Trust, Scotney Castle; Dr. John N. King, Ohio State University; Dr. Arthur F. Kinney, Jr., University of Massachusetts, Amherst; Rev. Robert Middlewick, Lamberhurst; Dr. Brooke Peirce, Goucher College; Ms. Niki Pollock, Special Collections, University of Glasgow Library; Ms. Sandra Rogge, London; Ms. P. D. Rowsby, The Centre for Kentish Studies, Maidstone; Dr. Lawrence V. Ryan, Stanford University; Dr. Harlow Sheidley, University of Colorado, Colorado Springs; Dr. John Thompson, The Queen's University of Belfast; and Mr. R. Woodhouse, Lamberhurst Local History Society. Special thanks are due to Professor John Manning, University of Wales, Lampeter, for help with the dissertation that has informed the introduction, and to Dr. David George, Urbana

University, Ohio, and Dr. Judith M. Kennedy, St. Thomas University, Fredericton, New Brunswick, both of whom carefully read the entire manuscript and provided many valuable suggestions.

Simon McKeown
King's College School, London

William E. Sheidley
University of Southern Colorado, Pueblo

Plate I

Jan Van der Noot, A *Theatre wherein be represented as wel the miseries & calamities that follow the voluptuous Worldlings, As also the greate ioys and plesures which the faithfull do enioy,* translated by Edmund Spenser (London: Henry Bynneman, 1569), B3.
By kind permission of The British Library.

INTRODUCTION

In 1569 the London printer William Seres, renowned mainly for producing books of prayers and devotions, published a slim octavo volume entitled *A newe Booke called the Shippe of safegarde.*[1] This work, ascribed on the title-page to one "G. B.," has the appearance of a poetic miscellany; in addition to a prose dedication, the volume includes an introductory address to the reader in fourteeners, two narrative versifications of miraculous incidents from a Latin redaction of Eusebius's *Ecclesiastical History,* and the long title-poem. In 219 ottava rima stanzas, plus a 36-line interpolation from the Chaucerian *Roman de la Rose,* "The Ship of safegarde," as the poem is headed in the text, is a moral and religious allegory in which man's life is likened to the passage of a ship through dangerous seas.[2] As the bark of man's life steers between islands, shoals, and whirlpools of sin towards its hoped-for destination, the Haven of Bliss, its pilot, the soul, must trust to the divine compass and card to negotiate a course through the dangers. The mariner must avoid the Rock of Pride, the Rock of Avarice, the Quicksands of Detraction, the Sandbanks of Gluttony, the Island of Fleshly Pleasure, the Rock of Heresy, the Island of Idolatry, and the Rock of Hypocrisy. Beset by such hazards, few ships achieve the blessed goal. Only the pilot who has safeguarded his ship with the bulwarks of piety and moral vigilance can reach the heavenly port. Once his ship is thus provisioned, helpful beacons such as Prayer, Peace, Love, Mercy, Patience, and Faith direct him towards the Haven of Bliss.

Traditional and generic as its theme might be, the poem is a representative mid-Tudor work, where the species of allegory is that of the sermon,

[1] The book is dated 1569 on its title page and was entered in the Stationers' Register for 1568–69.

[2] A thorough study of the journey motif within the Renaissance period is Samuel C. Chew, *The Pilgrimage of Life* (New Haven: Yale University Press, 1962).

in which the typically commonplace imagery is rarely allowed to distract from the deeply serious moral purpose of the author. Sometimes, however, the author indulges in a more sophisticated brand of allegory, in which the imagery is sustained and developed and made peculiarly appropriate to its context. In this vein "The Ship of safegarde" shows characteristics of later allegories like *The Faerie Queene*.[3] Typical also of the 1560s are both the poem's strong Protestant bias and its author's adaptation of stock imagery to promote a reformed agenda. Another distinctively Protestant feature of the poem is its use of polemic and satire to point up the follies and excesses of contemporary society. The poem thus suggests the influence of Erasmus's Lucianic satire as mediated through the mid-century English religious controversialists, notably John Bale. In addition, however, the poem reflects a wider intellectual commerce, as its author shows himself to be comfortable with both the milieu of neoclassical humanism and the doctrines of the early church fathers. There are also passages in the poem reminiscent of the conventions of the humanist emblem book. In detailing the Sandbanks of Gluttony and the Island of Fleshly Pleasure in particular, the imagery is highly visual, with the poet presenting a series of striking emblematic tableaux. This static rhetorical visualization, followed by close ecphrastic moralizing, resembles the *emblema nuda* species of emblem, where the *picturae* are replaced by verbal descriptions. In evidence too throughout the poem is that Horatian precept so popular with humanists in the sixteenth century, the pedagogic impulse to marry moral instruction and pleasant entertainment. For so long overlooked, *The Shippe of Safegarde*, for a range of reasons, is in need of modern reappraisal. It is hoped that the present edition will help facilitate a renewed interest in the work, thereby allowing the *Shippe* at last to assume its proper position on our rather short shelf of English literature from the 1560s.

The Author

As we have seen, Seres's 1569 edition of the *Shippe* attributes the work only to "G. B." Masking authors' names behind initials, inversions, and Latinized forms was common practice in the sixteenth century,[4] but in this case the authorial disguise was apparently enough to deceive even an attentive contemporary observer of the Elizabethan literary scene. In his *Discourse of English Poetrie* (1586), William Webbe mentions G. B., but seems to hold him distinct from the author modern scholars believe to

---

[3] For a discussion of the distinctions between these terms see Michael Murrin, *The Veil of Allegory* (Chicago: University of Chicago Press, 1969), 3–20.

[4] See two articles by Franklin Williams, "An Initiation into Initials," *Studies in Bibliography* 9 (1957): 163–78, and "Renaissance Names in Masquerade," *PMLA* 69 (1954): 314–23.

have written the *Shippe*, Barnabe Googe.[5] It is possible that Webbe was being fastidious about maintaining Googe's anonymity, but he may also have failed to link the *Shippe* with Googe because the book was little known and never reprinted in the decades following its publication. The obscurity of the *Shippe*'s provenance persisted into the eighteenth century when Thomas Warton omitted the text from his lengthy and admiring discussion of Googe's poetic career.[6] Although some subsequent authorities linked the volume with Googe, it was only in 1954 that the *Shippe* was accepted with certainty into the Googe canon, thanks to the work of Brooke Peirce, who demonstrated the extent to which the author of the *Shippe* shared common viewpoints, vocabulary, and stylistic idiosyncracies with Googe.[7] An analysis of the dedication confirmed Googe's authorship. The book is addressed to G. B.'s "verie good Sisters Mistresse Phillyp Darell, and Mistresse Fraunces Darell, of the house of Scotney," and is signed "Your loving brother in lawe." Barnabe Googe married Mary Darrell of Scotney Castle, Lamberhurst, Kent in 1564. The Darrell pedigree reveals that the only marriage between a daughter of Scotney and a spouse with the initials "G" and "B" was that between Googe and Mary.

Some further information can here be added. Although Peirce found references to a Mistress Fraunces Darrell in the archives relating to the family, he did not find any to her sister Phillyp, which, incidentally, was not an unusual female name at the time.[8] Mention is made of both sisters in the will of the girls' grandfather, Thomas Darrell, held in The Centre for Kentish Studies in Maidstone, dated 19 November 1557.[9] Proved in September of the following year, the will names Darrell's son Thomas—the girls' father—and his children, Harry, Alice, Mary, Phillip, and Frances. The specific bequest to the *Shippe*'s dedicatees is: "I geue to everrye of Phillip and FFraunces my Sonnes too othar daughters a heyfer of one yeres

[5] Webbe mentions G. B. in a list of minor authors, including John Grange and Francis Kinwelmersh. Earlier in his study he described Googe as a "painefull furtherer of learning" and noted his "helpe to Poetry besides hys owne deuices, as the translating of Pallengenius. Lodiac [sic]." See William Webbe, *A Discourse of English Poetrie*, edited by Edward Arber, English Reprints (London: Edward Arber, 1870), 34–35.

[6] See Thomas Warton, *History of English Poetry*, edited by W. Carew Hazlitt (London: Reeves & Turner, 1871), 4: 323–31.

[7] Early attributions are found in Sir Samuel Egerton Brydges and Joseph Haslewood, *The British Bibliographer* (London: R. Triphook, 1810–14), 2: 618–34; and A. H. Bullen, *Dictionary of National Biography*, edited by Leslie Stephen and Sidney Lee (London: Smith, Elder, 1890), 22: 151. Peirce's unpublished dissertation was the first full-length study devoted to Googe and remains essential reading for scholars in the field. For his discussion of the *Shippe*, see "Barnabe Googe: Poet and Translator" (Ph.D. diss., Harvard University, 1954), 178–214.

[8] Peirce, "Barnabe Googe: Poet and Translator," 202.

[9] The Centre for Kentish Studies, Maidstone, MS. U409 Z3.

age and uppwarde." The younger Thomas Darrell subsequently had two other daughters, Ellin and Margery. The fullest account of the daughters' various fates is found in the family pedigree given in the 1592 Visitation of Kent:

> After the saide Thomas maried to his seconde wiffe Marye Daughter and one of the heires of Thomas Royden of East Peckam Countie of Kent Esquire, and by her had issue Henrye his eldist sonne Edwarde or Edmonde, Thomas and Mathewe Dyed all sans issue Mary maried to Barnabye Goche of Alwingham in the Countie of Lyncolyn Esquire Frauncis maried to Roberte Grene of Bobbinge in the Countie of Kent gent Ellin maried to Edmonde Pelham of Catesfelde in the Countie of Sussex Esquire Margerye vnmaried, Margaret maried to Thomas Tyndall of Arlington in the Countie of Sussex gentilman.[10]

No mention is made of either Alice—recipient of bedding and a "white amblinge Maier" from her grandfather's estate—or Phillyp, both of whom we may assume died before 1592. Googe's acquaintance with the Darrells stemmed from his marriage and his close geographical proximity to Scotney Castle. Part of Mary Darrell's dowry was a farm at Chingley, a mile distant from the Darrell seat, and it was here that Googe and his new wife established their home.[11] Although Chingley lay in the neighboring parish of Ticehurst, many of Googe's activities were intimately linked to Lamberhurst and to Scotney. The parish not only saw his marriages, but also the baptisms of at least three of his children, and the burial of another child.[12] In later years Googe was involved in various legal transactions with the wider Darrell family, and was known as a prominent member of the gentry in that corner of Kent.[13] All in all, the evidence points overwhelmingly towards Googe as the author of the *Shippe*. The many and intimate links between Googe and the Darrells, together with the weight

---

[10] *The Visitation of Kent 1592*, Harleian Society 75 (1924), 94.

[11] We are grateful to Mr. Bob Woodham of the Lamberhurst Local History Society for providing this information taken from the notebooks of Rev. John Langhorne, antiquary and vicar of St. Mary's, Lamberhurst, 1893–1911.

[12] See John Moon, *A History of Lamberhurst* [England] (n.p., n.d.), 70.

[13] Mark Eccles notes one such transaction; see "Barnabe Googe in England, Spain, and Ireland," *English Literary Renaissance* 15 (1985): 353–70, 362. The Sussex Archaeological Society holds record of another action in 1578; see Courthope *Muniments Co/a 31* (1578). William Lambarde lists Googe as a member of the Kentish gentry in his *A Perambulation of Kent* (London: Henry Middleton f. Ralph Newbery, 1576), 56.

of internal evidence suggesting the pen of Googe, confirm that "G. B." was indeed Barnabe Googe.

Googe was an important pioneer of native English poetry in the mid-Tudor period.[14] Born on St. Barnabas's Day, 11 June 1540, he was the son of Robert Goche, a Lincolnshire retainer to several prominent figures within the Henrician and Edwardian reformist party, including Sir William Cecil—a distant relation of Goche—and Edward Seymour, Duke of Somerset and Lord Protector. Googe's mother died a month after his birth, and Googe, as was customary in such circumstances, was farmed out to the household of his maternal grandmother, Lady Hales of Dane John Manor, Canterbury. His treatment by Lady Hales was evidently kind; in later years Googe was to look back on her as "the very *Phoenix* and *Parageon* of al the Gentlewomen that I ever knewe."[15] Canterbury was the administrative center of the Church of England, and Dane John was renowned as a focal point for reformed thinkers within the city, attracting at various times such luminaries of the new faith as John Bale, Alexander Nowell, and Matthew Parker. Influential as the presence of such figures must have been on the development of Googe's religious and political outlook in his formative years, it was more probably an event typical of the vicissitudes of the mid-Tudor period that shaped his thinking along strongly Protestant lines. In 1554 Googe's stepgrandfather James Hales was arrested on religious grounds by the Marian authorities. While in prison, Hales, already mentally unstable, attempted suicide by cutting his wrists. He failed, but on his release a short time later, he threw himself into the River Stour near Canterbury and drowned.[16] This family tragedy, coupled with the testimony of the returning religious exiles at the end of Mary's reign, must have done much to convince Googe that the religious controversies of the day were manifestations of a forthright spiritual conflict

---

[14] The principal biographical and critical accounts of Googe are the following: Edward Arber, "Notes on the Life and Writings of Barnabe Googe" and "Introduction" to Googe, *Eglogs, Epytaphes and Sonettes (1563)*, edited by Arber, English Reprints (London: Edward Arber, 1871), 5–18; Peirce, "Barnabe Googe: Poet and Translator"; William E. Sheidley, *Barnabe Googe* (Boston: Twayne, 1981); Mark Eccles, "Barnabe Googe in England, Spain, and Ireland"; Judith M. Kennedy, "The Life and Times of Barnabe Googe" in Googe, *Eclogues, Epitaphs, and Sonnets*, edited by Kennedy (Toronto: University of Toronto Press, 1989), 3–16, 29–30; Judith M. Kennedy, "Googe, Barnabe," *The Spenser Encyclopedia*, edited by A. C. Hamilton et al. (Toronto: University of Toronto Press, 1990); Judith M. Kennedy, "Barnabe Googe," *Dictionary of Literary Biography, Volume 132: Sixteenth-Century British Nondramatic Writers, First Series* (Detroit: Gale Research, 1994), 141–48; and Simon McKeown, "Barnabe Googe: Poetry and Society in the 1560s" (Ph.D. diss., The Queen's University of Belfast, 1993).

[15] Conrad Heresbach, *Fovre Bookes of Husbandry*, translated by Barnabe Googe (London: Richard Watkins, 1577), X8.

[16] See Kennedy, "The Life," 5, and William Shakespeare, *Hamlet*, edited by Harold Jenkins, The Arden Shakespeare (London: Methuen, 1982), 547.

between good and evil. Googe's moral sternness and unremittingly bleak view of human nature may also have been informed by the physical location of Dane John within the city of Canterbury. Known locally as The Dungeon, Googe's childhood home overlooked the city's place of public execution, where Googe could have seen the rotting corpses of Protestant martyrs amongst the usual traffic of thieves and petty felons.

Googe's formal education was at Christ's College, Cambridge, an institution famous for its progressive theology in the sixteenth century, and alma mater of many English reformers. From Christ's, Googe proceeded to the Inns of Court in London and was a full participant in the burgeoning cultural life of that community. His first publication came at this time, when he was nineteen years old. The work, a poem of recommendation, prefaced Thomas Gressop's *A Briefe Treatise, Conteynynge a playne and fruitfull declaration of the Popes vsurped Primacye;* it appeared on 10 March 1560.[17] Of much greater importance was his next publication, which followed a fortnight later: his translation of the first three books of Marcellus Palingenius's *Zodiacus vitae*, a work first published in Venice in 1532.[18] Palingenius (alias Pietro Angelo Manzolli) was a poet under the patronage of Duke Ercole II D'Este of Ferrara. His *Zodiacus vitae* (or *The Zodiake of Life* in Googe's version) is a long moralizing satire on man's condition, encyclopedic in scope and occasionally brilliant in its imagery. The book had its controversial side, however; Palingenius was fully aware of the long-running enmity between the Estensi and the Papacy and included for Ercole's delight some passages satirizing both the Pope and the religious orders. Accordingly, in 1558 the *Zodiacus* was placed on the very first *Index librorum prohibitorum* and its late author exhumed and burned. This morbid posthumous fate did much to foster the view among reformed thinkers that Palingenius was a kind of crypto-Protestant, and his book enjoyed considerable success in reformed countries, often being reprinted at times of perceived Protestant peril, as in England in 1588 and the Netherlands in 1622. As a repository of memorable apophthegms and improving *sententiae*, the *Zodiacus* was valued for its educational potential,

---

[17] Nilus [Cabasilas], *A Briefe Treatise, Conteynynge a playne and fruitfull declaration of the Popes vsurped Primacye*, translated by Thomas Gressop (London: Henry Sutton f. Ralph Newbery, 1560).

[18] An excellent discussion of the work is Rosemond Tuve's introduction to Marcellus Palingenius Stellatus, *The Zodiake of Life*, translated by Barnabe Googe, edited by Rosemond Tuve (1947; Delmar, N.Y.: Scholars' Facsimiles & Reprints, 1976), v–xxvi. See also Foster Watson, *The "Zodiacus Vitae" of Marcellus Palingenius Stellatus: An Old Schoolbook* (London: Philip Wellby, 1908); Guiseppe Borgiani, *Marcello Palingenio Stellato e il suo poema lo "Zodiacus Vitae"* (Citto di Castello, 1912); Sheidley, *Barnabe Googe*, 28–47; J. M. Richardson, "Palingenius, Marcellus," *The Spenser Encyclopedia*, ed. Hamilton, 526; and McKeown, "Barnabe Googe: Poetry and Society," 129–82.

and in England it appeared on the statutes of several grammar schools.[19] Googe completed his task of translation in 1565 and furnished his work with an index and scholarly marginalia in 1576.[20] His endeavors in Englishing Palingenius earned Googe the high esteem of leading Protestant intellectuals, including Edward Dering, William Chadderton, and Abraham Fleming.[21]

Translating the *Zodiake* also gave Googe an opportunity to cultivate poet-patron relations with his now preeminent kinsman, Sir William Cecil. By the early 1560s Cecil was Elizabeth's chief minister. Of reformed bent, Cecil recognized the value of fostering the literary talents of his zealous young kinsman. This relationship was the most important connection in Googe's career. Through Cecil, Googe, whose father had died in 1558, was able to buy off his wardship at a favorable price;[22] through Cecil, Googe found regular employment at the households of Theobalds, Cecil House, and at Court;[23] through Cecil, Googe was able to sidestep obstacles placed in his way by Mary Darrell's parents when they suddenly entertained the overtures of a wealthier suitor;[24] through Cecil, Googe entered Parliament as M.P. for Aldeburgh in Yorkshire in 1571;[25] and through Cecil, Googe was employed on two spells of government duty in Ireland, one of which was an important military posting.[26] Googe repaid these favors with the fruits of his pen, presenting Cecil with successive editions of the *Zodiake* and relying on his patron's "learned protection and graue authority."[27] In 1579 he also dedicated to Cecil a translation of some Spanish moral proverbs of the Marquis of Santillana, and in 1577, aware of Cecil's affliction with gout, Googe tactfully dedicated to Richard

---

19 See Foster Watson, *The English Grammar Schools to 1660: Their Curriculum and Practice* (Cambridge: Cambridge University Press, 1908), 379.

20 Palingenius, *Zodiake* (London: Henry Denham f. Ralph Newbery, 1565); *Zodiake* (London: H. Middleton f. Ralph Newbery, 1576).

21 Prefatory matter, *Zodiake* (1565); *Zodiake* (1576), 242.

22 Eccles, "Barnabe Googe in England, Spain, and Ireland," 356.

23 Eccles, "Barnabe Googe in England, Spain, and Ireland," 362, 366, 370. See also Richard C. Barnett, *Place, Profit and Power: A Study of the Servants of William Cecil, Elizabethan Statesman* (Chapel Hill: University of North Carolina Press, 1969), 66–67.

24 The interesting correspondence concerning this affair is reprinted in Googe, *Eglogs, Epytaphes and Sonettes*, edited by Arber, 8–13.

25 Eccles, "Barnabe Googe in England, Spain, and Ireland," 363.

26 Details of Googe's duties and experiences in Ireland are vividly preserved in his dispatches to Cecil and other members of the Privy Council. These are printed in William Pinkerton, "Barnabe Googe," *Notes & Queries* 3rd Ser. 3 (1863): 141–43, 181–84, 241–43, 301–2, and 361–62. They are discussed in M. D. O'Sullivan, "Barnabe Googe: Provost Marshall of Connaught 1582–85," *Journal of the Galway Archaeological Society* 18 (1938): 1–39.

27 Epistle dedicatory, *Zodiake* (1565).

Masters, Cecil's physician, a slim medical poem detailing cures and salves for the disease.[28]

Probably Googe's most important literary venture—although it was not regarded as such in his lifetime—was the publication in March 1563, when he was twenty-two years old, of *Eglogs Epytaphes, and Sonettes*.[29] This small collection of original verse was unprecedented; no previous English author had published a volume of poems bearing his own name in his own lifetime. Although the collection shows its debt to *Tottel's Miscellany* of 1557, which was still very much in vogue, it has its own distinct points of interest. It boasts eight eclogues, which were among the earliest examples of original English pastoral. Sixteen years before the publication of Spenser's *Shepheardes Calender*, Googe was already handling moral, political, and religious questions under the cover of shepherds' songs. Of the volume's other pieces, the epitaphs, or elegies, are earnest and full of strong feeling, and the "sonettes," a miscellany of occasional verse, have been widely admired and anthologized over the past one hundred years.

In 1570, probably in response to Elizabeth's excommunication by Pope Pius V, Googe translated the *Regnum Papisticum* of Thomas Naogeorgus, or Kirchmeyer, a venomous satire on Roman folly and superstition.[30] Googe dedicated his *Popish Kingdome, or reign of antichrist*, to Elizabeth, hoping that she would find the work a "present meete for a Queene." In 1577 Googe translated a treatise on agriculture from the Latin of Conrad Heresbach, *Rei rusticae libri quatuor* (Cologne, 1570).[31] *Fovre Bookes of Husbandry* enjoyed many reprintings, and was still respected in 1634 when Gervase Markham produced a revision of Googe's text.[32] Although *Fovre Bookes* reflects its German origins, Googe was careful to augment his translation with additional information relevant to the English farmer. One detail is worth mentioning: in the prefatory materials Googe laments the

---

[28] Inigo Lopes de Mendoza, Marques of Santillana, *The Prouerbes . . .* , translated by Barnabe Googe (London: Richard Watkins, 1579); Christopher Ballista, *The Overthrow of the Gout*, trans. Barnabe Googe (London: Abraham Veale, 1577). For detailed studies of the latter see Robert M. Schuler, "Three Renaissance Scientific Poems," *Studies in Philology* 75,5 (1978): 65–107; and Ballista, *The Overthrow of the Gout*, translated by Barnabe Googe, edited by Simon McKeown (London: Indelible Inc., 1990).

[29] London: Thomas Colwell f. Raffe Newbery, 1563.

[30] Thomas Kirchmeyer, *The Popish Kingdome, or reign of Antichrist*, translated by Barnabe Googe (London: Henry Denham f. Richard Watkins, 1570). Googe's translation was reprinted in the nineteenth century, edited by Charles Hope (London: Chiswick Press, 1880), and in the facsimile reprint edited by Peter Davison (New York: Johnson Reprint Corporation, 1972). Googe may have been introduced to Kirchmeyer's work by John Bale, who was on familiar terms with the German reformer in the 1540s.

[31] See n.15, above.

[32] Conrad Heresbach, *The Whole Art of Husbandry*, translated by Barnabe Googe, revised by Gervase Markham (London: T. C. f. Richard More, 1631).

inability of the English at sustaining serious viniculture. Given that southern England enjoys the same meteorological conditions as the wine regions of Germany, Googe feels that Englishmen should be capable of producing palatable wine. It is a testimony to Googe's agricultural acuity and intuition that his home parish of Lamberhurst now contains England's most productive vineyard.

The year 1587 saw Googe's last published work, another translation, this time from a Latin work (Frankfurt, 1583) by Andreas Berthold.[33] In this odd little book Googe preaches the virtues of a supposed wonder drug, *Terra Sigillata*. The prose dedication, addressed again to Masters, and another physician, Dr. Baylie, was signed from Alvingham in Lincolnshire. Googe had moved in the mid-1580s from Kent to his family seat, and passed his time in obscure retirement until his death in February 1594.

By the time of his death, Googe had earned wide respect as the translator of Palingenius and Heresbach, but was largely forgotten as an original poet. By the mid 1590s, readers had before them examples of the work of Spenser, Sidney, and Marlowe. Googe's original work from the 1560s belonged to a different era and must have seemed hopelessly outmoded in comparison to the flurry of sonnet sequences and elegant lyrics which were tripping from the presses. Googe's favored meter, the fourteener, a native approximation to the classical alexandrine, had once been regarded as a powerful tool of didactic expression. Now it had become a byword for rustic uncouthness: Shakespeare's Rude Mechanicals in *A Midsummer Night's Dream* hope to have the prologue to their amateur dramatics "written in eight and six."[34] There can be no doubt that the historical proximity of Googe and other sober-minded writers of the mid-Tudor period to the glittering latter decades of the sixteenth century has done little to enhance their reputation. It should be remembered, however, that this earlier generation of writers did much to prepare the way for the later successes of the English literary Renaissance. They created a climate where literary production came to be respected and praised. For the greater glory of the English tongue they conscientiously naturalized a range of classical and continental models and provided the unlearned with serviceable vernacular versions of seminal texts. Thus they familiarized a native audience with literary forms and educated them in styles and conventions that later writers could build upon. Laboring against the censure of a received wisdom that branded English verse as barbarous, Googe and his contempora-

---

[33] Andreas Bertholdus, *The Wonderful and strange effect and vertues of a new Terra Sigillata lately found out in Germanie*, translated by Barnabe Googe (London: Robert Robinson f. Richard Watkins, 1587).

[34] William Shakespeare, *A Midsummer Night's Dream*, edited by Harold F. Brooks, The Arden Shakespeare (London: Methuen, 1979), 3.1.23.

ries improvised a vernacular poetry from an eclectic range of models. *The Shippe of safegarde* typifies this cultural acquisitiveness. It is at once deeply traditional and yet forward-looking, morally urgent yet iconoclastic, conventional yet idiosyncratic. In all, the *Shippe* exemplifies much of the English literary achievement of the mid-Tudor years. In both its strengths and its limitations it provides evidence of a burgeoning faith in the native cultural voice while further revealing many of the confusions and contradictions that cut across that politically and religiously uncertain society.

The Imagery of "The Ship of Safegarde": Traditions and Analogues

The notion that life is like a voyage is, arguably, the paradigmatic metaphor for human existence.[35] The concept occurs in nearly all cultures in all ages, found in such varied expressions as Egyptian and Norse after-life beliefs, biblical episodes such as those of Noah and Jonah, Indian and Arabian tales of Sinbad, and Homer's *Odyssey*. As Hans Blumenberg has recently explained, "the repertory of this nautical metaphorics of existence is very rich. It includes coasts and islands, harbors and the high seas, reefs and storms, shallows and calms, sail and rudder, helmsmen and anchorages, compass and astronomical navigation, lighthouses and pilots."[36] Whether human life is comfortable and secure, or troubled and vexed, the marine figure provides humanity with a spectrum of images to express its condition. And as Blumenberg noted, "the metaphorics of embarkation includes the suggestion that living means already being on the high seas, where there is no outcome other than being saved or going down, and no possibility of abstention."[37]

Given the ubiquity of the theme, one hesitates to claim with any confidence the ultimate source or inspiration for Googe's poem. There are, however, certain texts and traditions from which he clearly draws. The most obvious is Homer's *Odyssey*, not least because Googe cites episodes and incidents from the epic at various points of his poem. Googe could have read the *Odyssey* in a Latin translation, a number of which had been published during the first half of the sixteenth century, but the stories he refers to were commonly found in *compendia* and *florilegia*, and it may have been such a collection that furnished him with details from the poem. It

---

[35] In addition to Chew, *Pilgrimage of Life*, see W. H. Auden, *The Enchafèd Flood or the Romantic Iconography of the Sea* (New York: Random House, 1950); Robert Cockcroft, *The Voyage of Life: Ship Imagery in Art, Literature and Life* (Nottingham: University of Nottingham Art Gallery, 1982); and Philip Edwards, *Sea-Mark: The Metaphorical Voyage, Spenser to Milton*, Liverpool English Texts & Studies 30 (Liverpool: University of Liverpool, 1997).

[36] Hans Blumenberg, *Shipwreck with Spectator: Paradigm of a Metaphor for Existence*, translated by Steven Rendall (Cambridge, Mass.: MIT Press, 1997), 7.

[37] Blumenberg, *Shipwreck with Spectator*, 19.

is, of course, entirely unsurprising to find a Christian poet of this period reconfiguring pagan material to suit a Christian theme. Homer was among those ancient writers who were felt to be divinely enlightened and whose works contained covert Christian instruction. Medieval and Renaissance readers interpreted the Homeric epics as moral and religious allegories of human life, and episodes and incidents from them were subjected to close typological analysis.[38]

Googe, though, did not have to resort to Christianized readings of the ancients to find the theme of his poem because biblical and Christian literature made extensive use of the ship and sea motifs. Men and women of Googe's era must have been very familiar with the comparison of man's life to a voyage, and of the ship as a place of refuge in a precarious world. In the Elizabethan *Boke of Common Praier* of 1559, the Divine Service for Baptism asks the Lord that the children "maye be receaued into the Arke of Christes Churche: and beeynge stedfaste in faythe, ioyefull through hope, and rooted in charitie, may so passe the waues of this troublesome worlde, that finally they maye come to the lande of euerlastyng lyfe, there to reygne with thee. . . ."[39] It could be that Googe found the key inspiration for his poem from the Anglican liturgy, but as a literary man he must also have been conscious of a range of other sources. He may have known, for example, the Legend of St. Brandan from Wynkyn de Worde's *Golden Legend* of 1527.[40] The story details the holy man's seven years of voyaging and his encounters with bejewelled islands and fabulous fish. The narrative structure is to a large extent dependent on the turning of the Church calendar, and the tale's moral impact is made through the emphasis placed on the saint's godly and estimable life. Googe likely also knew Chaucer's story of the morally pure Custance in the "Man of Law's Tale" from *The Canterbury Tales*,[41] which features prolonged voyaging sequences and includes the motif of the charmed or magical boat so popular in Romance literature. The story's purpose, however, is much more elaborate than the typical Romance, and the tale of Custance and her voyages has considerable allegorical significance. The tale comes to speak of no-

---

[38] For a discussion of the moral gloss imposed by Renaissance readers on classical writers, see Douglas Bush, *Mythology and the Renaissance Tradition in English Poetry* (Minneapolis: University of Minnesota Press, 1932), 68ff.

[39] *The Boke of common praier, and administration of the Sacramentes, and other rites and Ceremonies in the Churche of Englande* (London: Richard Grafton, 1559), S1^{v}–S2^{r}.

[40] The tale is reprinted in *St. Brandan, a Medieval Legend of the Sea*, edited by Thomas Wright (London: Percy Society, 1844).

[41] An excellent study of the tale, and a thorough discussion of the nautical motif in Christian iconography, is V. A. Kolve, *Chaucer and the Imagery of Narrative* (London: Edward Arnold, 1984), 297–358.

tions of life and death, rebirth and renewal, and separation and restoration, as well as providing images of the sacraments and the nature of the Christian life. Custance's obedience, faith, and perseverance can be read as exemplary patterns of pious behavior, and of direct application in righteous living. The ship in which she drifts connects with ancient ideas of the Ship of the Church, with Providence at the helm. The seas are the trials of life, and the destination the port of heaven. On this allegorical level, the story of Custance inhabits the same imaginative world as Googe's "Ship" and makes use of similar iconographic conventions. Googe is no hagiographer, however, and the "Ship" differs in important ways from both the stories of Custance and St. Brandan. These tales have a happy resolution, and the tensions created by the various situations and states experienced by the protagonists are relieved. In Googe's voyage the central protagonist is essentially Everyman, and the outcome of his journey remains uncertain: success depends on the mariner's following the navigational principles mediated by Googe from scriptural authority. The resolution of the issues raised in the poem lies outside the work, in the individual conscience of the reader.

In its allegoresis of moral choice and appeal to the reader's conscience, the "Ship" employs features of another religious literary form. The homiletic tradition, variously expressed in sermons, biblical commentaries, and works of devotion, had been a major channel of religious discourse from the earliest days of the Christian faith, and remained undiminished in its stature and popularity in the sixteenth century. The homilist viewed himself as a humble interlocutor between Christ's message and the common believer, and this role of advocate and teacher often required the use of mundane metaphors to illustrate profound spiritual mysteries. The homilist used images from everyday experience, and it is not surprising to find the image of the storm-tossed ship as one of the commonest metaphors used in homiletic writing. Examples among the works of the early church fathers are numerous and seem to have their roots in a range of biblical episodes such as Noah and the Deluge or Christ's calming of the storm. In his *Sermons*, St. Augustine figured the church as a ship sailing on the seas of temptation, beset by winds and dangers.[42] Of greater interest to the reader of Googe, however, are the works of St. John Chrysostom, fourth-century Bishop of Constantinople. Like other homilists, he compares the virtuous man, for example, to "a skilful pilot, controlling the rudder of his mind with great vigilance, not allowing the craft to be submerged under the volume of the billows of wickedness, but getting the better of the storm and riding it out at sea as though safely berthed in

---

[42] Kolve, *Chaucer and the Imagery of Narrative*, 314.

port."[43] Elsewhere he compares the Christian's desire of heaven to the avarice of the seafaring merchant.[44] From allusions in the prefatory matter to the 1565 edition of the *Zodiake* we know that Googe had read and admired Chrysostom's works by the time he wrote the *Shippe*.[45] Chrysostom was widely regarded as a venerable champion of simple, unadorned Christianity, and his works enjoyed great popularity among reformers. Of all the early church fathers, sixteenth-century Protestants found the doctrines of Chrysostom to be most in harmony with their own beliefs. Thus in 1543, John Cheke in seeking to encourage Henry VIII in the role of the reformist prince presented him with an edition of Chrysostom's works.[46]

By the Middle Ages, the influence of generations of homiletic writers had made the ship motif a commonplace for life's perils and trials. As G. R. Owst has shown, in the pulpit the basic image was subjected to almost endless elaborations and refinements.[47] It could take on the form of the universal church or the individual mortal. Sometimes the ship's mast figured as the cross of Christ, and the wind that filled the sails the inspiration of the Holy Ghost. In other versions, sins in the forms of sea-monsters could assail the ship or the vessel could be pitched by the storms of Pride. Attuned to these subtle variations on the theme, the Renaissance reader of homilies continued to be drawn by the imaginative appeal of the ship image. Numerous books of meditations from the period take as a starting point the similitude of life as a voyage.[48] Usually, however, the nautical image does not extend far beyond the title; the image serves as a springboard for more general religious reflections. An instance of this is

---

[43] St. John Chrysostom, *Homilies on Genesis*, translated by Robert C. Hill, The Fathers of the Church (Washington, D.C.: Catholic University of America Press, 1990), 82: 87.

[44] St. John Chrysostom, *On the Incomprehensible Nature of God*, translated by Paul W. Harkins, The Fathers of the Church (Washington, D.C.: Catholic University of America Press, 1984), 72: 185.

[45] Prefatory matter, *Zodiake* (1565), *8^{v}, (‡)2^{v}–(‡)3.

[46] Joannis Chrysostomi, *Homilae duae*, translated by John Cheke (London: R. Wolfe, 1543).

[47] See G. R. Owst, *Literature and the Pulpit in Medieval England*, 2nd ed. (1933; Oxford: Basil Blackwell, 1966), 67–76, 177–78.

[48] See for example Edward Cradocke, *The shippe of assured safetie* (London: William Norton, 1572); A. P., *The Compasse of a Christian. Directing them that be tossed in the waues of this worlde vnto Christ Iesus* (London: J. Wolfe f. J. Harison the younger, 1582); John Hull, *The Arte of christian saylinge* (London: J. Harrison & S. Stafford f. J. Harison, 1602); Richard Middleton, *Card and Compasse of life . . .* (London: W. S. f. Walter Burre, 1613); James Pickford, *The safegarde from ship-wracke or heaven's haven* (Douai: Peter Telv, 1618); Thomas Odell, *A brief and short treatise. Called The Christians Pilgrimage to His Fatherland* (Amsterdam: John Fredericksz, 1635); Thomas Brewer, *Lord have mercy upon us . . .* (London: Henry Gosson, 1636); Jeremiah Burroughs, *The sea mans direction in time of storme* (London: T. Paine & M. Simmons, 1640); Thomas Elsliot, *The true mariner and his pixis nautical* (London: s.n., 1652).

Stephen Bateman's *A christall glasse of christian reformation* (1569), which announces its homily on Hope with an allegorical woodcut that dramatizes the Christian life as a passage through stormy seas. The text of the homily proper, however, makes no further allusion to marine imagery.[49] Metaphors in homiletic literature are not drawn out to the lengths achieved in the "Ship," where Googe tries to couch his moral lessons in literary artifice. It is his intention, as he states in the dedication, to delight as well as to instruct, and to this end his precepts and sober guidance are enlivened by the imaginative development of the ship figure.

The "Ship," then, does not seem particularly indebted to any one literary precedent, but rather draws on several venerable traditions. The fusion of literary genres within Googe's book has led John N. King to see the "Ship," together with Stephen Bateman's *The Travayled Pylgrime*, as exemplifying "Elizabethan syncretism," where authors brought together an "encyclopedic combination of romance, quest narrative, didactic allegory, and Protestant polemics."[50] But whereas establishing connections with earlier works is problematic, no such difficulty exists when seeking resemblances between the "Ship" and later works. A little over a month after Googe dedicated the *Shippe* to the Darrell sisters, Edmund Spenser made his first appearance in print as the precocious translator of verses in Jan Van der Noot's *A Theatre for Voluptuous Worldlings*.[51] Among Spenser's contributions to *A Theatre* is a series of epigrammatic translations from Petrarch, mediated to Spenser through Clément Marot's *De Visions de Pétrarque*. The second epigram describes the fate of a magnificent and richly laden ship which founders on a submerged rock when a "sodaine storme did ... turmoyle the aire, / And tombled up the sea. ..." For Petrarch, and Spenser, the vision of a stricken ship suggests the fragility of human ambitions and the dangers of presumption. Spenser was to enlarge upon the theme of a moralized voyage years later when he described Guyon's passage to the Bower of Bliss in Book II of *The Faerie Queene*. The description of the Bower itself shares striking parallels with Googe's Island of Fleshly Pleasure. The Rocks of Avarice, littered with the wealth of shipwrecked souls, recall Spenser's "Rich strond" in Book III, and the ship's progress past a series of allegorical temptations has points of contact

---

[49] Stephen Bateman, *A christall glasse of christian reformation wherein the godly maye beholde the coloured abuses vsed in this our present tyme* (London: John Day, 1569), N3.

[50] See John N. King, *Spenser's Poetry and the Reformation Tradition* (Princeton, N.J.: Princeton University Press, 1990), 5.

[51] Jan Van der Noot, *A Theatre wherein be represented as wel the miseries & calamities that follow the voluptuous Worldlings, As also the greate ioyes and plesures which the faithfull do enioy* (London: Henry Bynneman, 1569). See *The Yale Edition of the Shorter Poems of Edmund Spenser*, ed. William A. Oram et al. (New Haven: Yale University Press, 1989), 465.

with the parade of the Seven Cardinal Sins in Book I. There is little evidence to suggest that Spenser was directly indebted to Googe's poem, or indeed that he was even familiar with the piece, although the two poets may have met in Ireland in the early 1580s.[52] Spenser certainly did not require the example of Googe's allegory to spur on his own fecund imagination, but it is nonetheless instructive to compare the diverse angles of approach between the two poets when handling similar themes. Another major work from a later period also derives from the same broad tradition as Googe's "Ship." John Bunyan's *The Pilgrim's Progress* (1678 & 1684) is arguably the definitive expression of the spiritual journey theme in English literary culture.[53] Although the "Ship" again falls short of the complexity and profundity of Bunyan's classic rendering of the Puritan experience, the two works have much in common. Both hinge upon the journey metaphor; both portray life as a succession of challenges and dangers; and both are driven by the conviction that continence and discipline are requisite for a successful negotiation of life's trials. Both even share a taste for embodying abstract notions with concrete forms: Googe with his Rock of Pride or Channel of Lowliness, Bunyan with his Slough of Despond and the Delectable Mountains. Important distinctions remain between "The Ship of safegarde" and works of the calibre of *The Pilgrim's Progress* and *The Faerie Queene*. The "Ship" links each poetic description—in itself usually a success—with a protracted exposition and interpretation. Spenser and Bunyan present their material in the enigmatic and resonant splendor of allegory proper, rarely intruding to offer commentaries on their conceits. *The Faerie Queene*, despite its vastness, maintains an internal coherence and unity, and its allegory is sustained, consistent, and suggestive. *The Pilgrim's Progress*, a simpler allegorical narrative, nonetheless remains similarly clear, focused, and monolithic in form and intent. In these areas the "Ship" is deficient. The allegorical structure repeatedly breaks down with digressions, anecdotes, and multifarious allusions. Even Googe himself sometimes seems unsure of his exact allegorical intentions: the ship itself can be read variously as representing the individual soul, or body, or mortal man collectively.

These confusions are symptomatic of the poem's mixed origins and intentions. Cross-bred with the various strains of homily, legend, allegory, and spiritual biography, the "Ship" on the whole emulates none of these forms at their best, and can appear to lack refinement and grace. In common with other mongrel breeds, however, the poem abounds in spirit and

[52] See Kennedy, "Googe, Barnabe," *The Spenser Encyclopedia*, ed. Hamilton, 336–37, 336.

[53] A useful survey of Bunyan's sources is James Blanton Wharey, *A Study of the Sources of Bunyan's Allegories* (Baltimore: J. H. Furst, 1904; repr., New York: Gordian Press, 1968).

vigor. And this is its real significance; for a literary culture so long lying moribund and uninspired, the "Ship" and works of its kind offered evidence that in the early years of Elizabeth's reign a new pride and confidence in English letters was abroad, and with it a new mood of experimentation among native poets.

The Circumstances of Googe's Dedication

Googe chose to dedicate *The Shippe of Safegarde* to his sisters-in-law on St. Valentine's Day. A tradition of the sixteenth century dictated that on the 14th of February men and women of all ages drew random names from a hat to determine their Valentine for the day. The practice, and its potential for disaster, is humorously described in Googe's poem "Of the Unfortunate Choice of his Valentine."[54] Both married and unmarried alike entered into this game; if a married partner were chosen, he or she could be absolved of amorous obligations by presenting a gift to the choosing party. The formal occasion of the *Shippe*'s dedication to the Darrell sisters may have stemmed from this seasonal tradition, but in his epistle Googe says he had long intended to present the girls with a book. Considering their "vertuous and well disposed minds" in their "yong and tender yeares"—judging by their grandfather's will they must have been at least twelve years old at the time—Googe resolved to show his good will towards them by "finding out such matter, as neither I might accompt my time vainly spent in wryting, nor you yours evill employed in reading." He had settled on a project seeking to delineate "the perfite estate of a true christian," and had given it the working title of "the counterfeyt Christian," but his nearly completed manuscript met with "yll favourd misfortune." Dismayed by the loss of his labors, Googe hastily began the *Shippe* "with a scarse quiet mind." He explains that the conceit was inspired by his reflecting on the "daungers of this worlde, whereby the soule enclosed in the barke of sinfull fleshe wyth great hasard passeth," though he confesses that the end product of his work is "a Ship but rudely furnished, and God knowes symply rygged." Because the girls "delight in stories," he has appended two tales from the lives of saints of the early church. He would have added more, but found his time pressured and the tales "tedious." All this, of course, is the standard gracious rhetoric of dedications, where the writer plays down his literary ability, the charge of presumption is countered by the insistence of a moral purpose, and the product of long careful hours is dismissed as a trifle. Aside from his kinship by marriage to

[54] The custom is described in R. Chambers, *The Book of Days: A Miscellany of Popular Antiquities* (London: W. & R. Chambers, 1863), 1: 255. For Googe's poem, see *Eclogues*, ed. Kennedy, 98.

the Darrells, it was natural for Googe to dedicate his book to two such adolescents: it was a practice of ancient pedigree to present improving works for the edification and delight of minors. What makes Googe's choice of dedication particularly interesting in the case of the *Shippe* is that he was directing his work at the daughters of a recusant household.[55]

Fraunces and Phillyp's grandfather had not only been the lord of the manor of Scotney, but also is said to have served as priest in the parish church of St. Mary's, Lamberhurst, from 1547.[56] He did not live to see the accession of Elizabeth, but just two months prior to her coronation he bequeathed to his son Thomas his beloved instruments and paraphernalia of devotion, including mass books, psalters, a chalice, vestments, candlesticks, cruets, and a sacring bell. Other references in his will show him to have been a considerable benefactor to the churches in that part of the Kentish Weald. He arranged for Lamberhurst's benefice to be repaired, and he made provision for the proper dressing of the altars in the parish churches of Wadhurst, Ticehurst, and Goudhurst. With the Elizabethan ecclesiastical settlement of 1559, Thomas Darrell the younger maintained the family's adherence to the old faith. Although nothing is explicitly stated in the documents relating to Googe's courtship wrangles with the family, it seems most likely that Darrell's low estimate of the poet was influenced by the latter's connections with such figures as Cecil and Parker. For a range of reasons, Darrell must have balked at the notion of establishing kinship with such a well-connected and energetic advocate of reformed thought.

In time, Thomas Darrell's recusancy extended beyond a mere refusal to adopt Anglican forms of worship. Soon after the first Jesuit missionaries arrived in England from Cardinal Allen's seminary at Douai (about 1573), Darrell offered Scotney as a safe house for incoming priests.[57] As such it was ideally situated. Scotney is an inconspicuous and relatively small manorial house, nestling in a large hollow, where even as late as the eighteenth century the air was felt to be unhealthy.[58] In Googe's time the surrounding terrain was heavily wooded, and in places marshy.[59] Despite its seclusion, however, it lay near the London-to-Rye road, thus affording

---

55 The Darrells' recusancy is noted in Peirce, "Barnabe Googe: Poet and Translator," 203–5, and Kennedy, "The Life," 30.

56 See William Morland, *The Church in Lamberhurst* ([England]: n.p., 1978), 13. Morland does not explain the apparent conflict between grandfatherhood and celibacy.

57 See John Morris, *The Troubles of Our Catholic Forefathers* (London: n.p., 1872), 2: 187–215.

58 See Christopher Hussey, *Scotney Castle* (London: The National Trust, 1990), 21.

59 The woodland, now partially cleared, provided fuel for iron-smelting, the area's principal industry in the early modern period. See Hussey, *Scotney Castle*, 3.

easy access to either the capital or the English Channel. In short, Scotney was an excellent staging-post for incoming Jesuit missionaries. Darrell's commitment to the cause was so great that in 1580, while refurbishing the south wing of the castle, he fitted a network of concealed hiding-places—which can still be seen—alongside the grand oak staircase added also at this time. His clandestine activities at Scotney passed undetected until 1598 when the castle was twice searched after a Protestant serving-man tipped off the authorities.[60] The object of the searches was the renowned Jesuit Richard Blount, who had been installed at Scotney since 1591. Holed up for ten days while the searches took place around him, the priest made a dramatic escape over the frozen moat and the surrounding rough terrain, but the authorities arrested Thomas Darrell on suspicion of harboring Jesuit missionaries. He was taken to London and imprisoned in Newgate; his name disappears from the records at this point, and it is thought that Thomas Darrell died in custody.[61]

These events lay some time in the future when Googe dedicated the *Shippe* to Thomas Darrell's daughters in 1569. There can be no doubt that when he did so he was well aware of the family's religious leanings. Quite aside from his intimate and established knowledge of the family and their affairs, his mere domicile in the Lamberhurst area would have afforded him every opportunity to ascertain something of the Darrells' heterodoxy on religious matters, their secret being so open that one anonymous clerk recorded in the parish register of the burial of Mary's aunt as being "early in the morning without knowledge of the Minister and without Divine service."[62] It is worth noting that despite intermittent harassment the Darrell family kept true to Catholicism until the line expired in the late eighteenth century.[63] For Googe the gulf between his opinions and those of his wife's family must have seemed unbridgeable. As an ardent reformer, Googe would have found Darrell's recusancy and the Roman influence presumably exerted over his household deeply repugnant; due to the bonds of blood and civility, however, he was compelled to leave his extended family unmolested. His apparent response to this quandary was characteristic. Convinced of the efficacy of the written word to challenge and persuade the unreformed, Googe penned *The Shippe of Safegarde* as a shot in the polemical battle over the intellectual and emotional territory of his sisters-in-law. The *Shippe* is not, however, an overtly controversial text. Indeed by the standards of the day, it is restrained: in seeking to communi-

---

60 See Morris, *Troubles of Our Catholic Forefathers*, 207–11.

61 Morris, *Troubles of Our Catholic Forefathers*, 231; Hussey, *Scotney Castle*, 12.

62 Morland, *The Church in Lamberhurst*, 13.

63 Hussey, *Scotney Castle*, 16.

cate reformed notions to his Catholic in-laws, Googe's approach was insinuative rather than incendiary.

Nonetheless, a Protestant ethos pervades the work. The emphasis throughout is on the centrality of scriptural authority. Googe's deployment of biblical exempla both familiarized the girls with biblical episodes and demonstrated to them the usefulness of scriptural exegesis in the sphere of personal morality. Repeated use of the Bible also absolved Googe from censure, as his arguments were conspicuously grounded on scripture. On some issues, though, Googe more obviously raised his head above the Protestant parapet. In the section dealing with Heresy, for example, Googe turns on the opponents of the vernacular Bible, dismissing them as "envious beasts" driven by "malice" (st. 152). This attack on the enemies of the English Bible coincided almost exactly with the publication and distribution of the new Bishop's Bible, that peculiarly Anglican translation commissioned and regulated by Matthew Parker.[64] Elizabeth and Cecil had reviewed the finished work on 22 September 1568, and it was put to press shortly thereafter. Published with a frontispiece portrait of Elizabeth herself, and also carrying full-page xylographs of Cecil and Dudley, the Bishop's Bible was a potent symbol of Protestant political and ideological dominance in 1560s England.[65] Among the prefatory materials, Parker reprinted the prologue Thomas Cranmer had originally added to the Great Bible of Henry VIII's reign. There Cranmer sought, in imagery later to be used by Googe, to encourage a public unused to the notion of free access to the scriptures: "They that be free and farre from trouble and entermedling of worldly thynges liue in safegarde and tranquilitie, and in the calme, or within a sure hauen. Thou art in the middest of the sea of worldly wyckednesse, and therefore thou needest the more of ghostly succour and comfort."[66] In the "Ship" Googe clearly endorses the aims and aspirations of the ongoing translation movement. In stanza 153 he ridicules the efforts of an unnamed individual who recently

> needlesse paines did take
> In culling out the faults he could espie,
> Of everie tittell straight accompt doth make
> In noting where he thinkes [the translators] run awrie.

The subject of this attack is uncertain, but Googe is obviously alluding to a known enemy of Bible translation who had identified perceived heresies

[64] See F. F. Bruce, *The History of the Bible in English* (London: Lutterworth, 1970), 92–95.

[65] See Margaret Aston, *The King's Bedpost: Reformation and Iconography in a Tudor Group Portrait* (Cambridge: Cambridge University Press, 1993), 43–47, 124, 133.

[66] Prefatory matter, *The holie bible*, 2nd ed. (London: Richard Jugge, 1572).

and errors in the translators' work. One figure that fits the description is Stephen Gardiner, Bishop of Winchester, and a conservative churchman under Henry, Edward, and Mary. In 1542 he had pronounced the Great Bible "contaminate, sometime ... with the malice of the translator ... sometime by ignorance and sometime by negligence."[67] The list of words he felt defied appropriate translation into the common tongue included many basic religious terms such as *Christus*, *Dominus*, *sacramentum*, *gratia*, *charitas*, and *mysterium*.[68] To reformed eyes, the exclusion of such vocabulary precluded the usefulness of a translation to the unlearned, and could merit Googe's estimation of his target's labors as the fruits of a "fonde and foolish braine."

Other passages in the poem reveal its Protestant stance. In the treatment of Idolatry, Googe envisions an alluring island adorned with pyramids and altars and dotted with scented fires (sts. 161–69). He describes some of the many statues and graven images to be found there, and among them lists those of Saturn, Venus, Mars, Diana, Bacchus, Ceres, and other deities from the classical pantheon. He then proceeds to describe three other statues, the first two recognizable by their attributes as St. George and St. Christopher. The third image, that of an androgynous trifrons, would seem to be a representation of the demonic Hecate. Googe thus equates the veneration of such talismanic Christian saints as St. George and St. Christopher with the worship of the pagan gods, including that of witchcraft.

This uncompromising but oblique presentation of reformed opinions is carried on in the patristic translations Googe appended to his title poem. The stories are taken from the standard Renaissance edition of Eusebius's *Ecclesiastical History*, a Latin version originally compiled in the fifth century by Rufinus Tyrannius. Rufinus had freely but silently altered his material, grafting additional tales and incidents onto Eusebius's text, and Googe's second tale is one of these spurious additions.[69] The first passage tells of the martyrdom of St. Polycarp, Bishop of Smyrna.[70] This story of the immolation of an early church martyr suggests that Googe was attuned

[67] Cited in James Arthur Muller, *Stephen Gardiner and the Tudor Reaction* (London: Society for Promoting Christian Knowledge, 1926), 105.

[68] Muller, *Stephen Gardiner*, 104–5.

[69] See Sheidley, *Barnabe Googe*, 101. Rufinus's translation, edited by Theodore Mommsen, appears on facing pages with the Greek original in Eusebius, *Kirchengeschichte*, ed. Eduard Schwartz, 3 vols., cont. pag. (Leipzig: J. C. Hinrichs, 1903–9), hereinafter cited as Rufinus.

[70] For the original account, see Eusebius, *The History of the Church*, translated by G. A. Williamson, edited by Andrew Louth (London: Penguin, 1989), 118–23, and Eusebius, *Ecclesiastical History*, translated by Kirsopp Lake, vol. 1, Loeb Classical Library (London: Heinemann, 1926), 343–57. See also Rufinus, 339–53.

to the interest such accounts carried with a public inspired by John Foxe's *Acts and Monuments of These Latter and Perilous Days*. More commonly known as Foxe's *Book of Martyrs*, this work, first published in 1563, was a formidable memorial to the Protestant martyrs who had suffered persecution under Mary Tudor. Googe's translation is on the whole faithful to his original, but it is the details where he differs from Eusebius and Rufinus that are of real interest. Googe's account is more succinct and direct than the original: gone are the latter's digressions and elaborations. In part this simplification of the text could result from Googe's effort to keep the interest of the young readers to whom the work is addressed. But Googe does not merely edit Eusebius. He adds phrases and emphases to the existing text, and in places inserts blocks of his own verse. Accordingly the account of Polycarp's martyrdom takes on new color. The opening fourteen lines are entirely Googe's, serving as an introduction to the action of Eusebius's account by recalling the widespread persecution of the early church. The persecutors are described as descending on the "Christian flocke" with "wolvish tongue and tooth." Googe is here connecting with a standard metaphor of the Reformation struggle in which the sheep represent the reformers, innocent creatures of God's flock, and the wolf represents Rome, the ravenous agent of the devil. Googe thus looks back not only to terrible and momentous events of the second century A.D., but also to those of recent memory. It is no accident that the story of Polycarp tells of a Greek bishop suffering at the hands of Roman authorities; reformers across Europe saw themselves as the heirs of the simple faith espoused by the primitive Greek Church.[71] Like these early followers of Christ, they also found themselves to be a minority community undergoing persecution. In some particulars, however, the Polycarp story was not wholly suitable as an ideal Protestant biography. Googe felt it necessary to deflect attention away from Polycarp himself for fear of encouraging idolatry, and to focus instead on the worthiness of his beliefs. Thus the role of the portentous dream in the account is underplayed, and the marvels attendant on Polycarp's death are summarily handled. In Eusebius, the reader is provided with a mystical appreciation of the dead martyr's broken body, the bones being weighed "more precious than stones of great price, more splendid than gold."[72] Googe omits the passage entirely and replaces it with a more spiritual evaluation of Polycarp's death: "The people all amased, depart, the corse neglected lies, / The soule rejoycing at this day,

---

[71] See Philip Edgcumbe Hughes, *The Theology of the English Reformers* (London: Hodder & Stoughton, 1965), 30ff.

[72] Eusebius, trans. Williamson, 122; cf. Eusebius, translated by Lake, 357.

unto the heaven flies" (ll. 206–7). The bishop's body is "neglected," having served its mortal purpose; Googe thus precludes its use as an object of veneration.

The second story, one of Rufinus's additions to Eusebius,[73] affords similar contemporary applications. It recounts the tale of Gregory, Bishop of Neocaesarea, who converts a votary of Apollo by a demonstration of the true God's power.[74] Here again, the story seems handpicked by Googe for the instruction of his sisters-in-law. It shows the redundancy of worshipping false gods and the superiority of the Christian God to all other deities. The spiritual wealth of Gregory stands in contradistinction to the material splendor of the priest's "gorgeous temple faire" (l. 2), illustrating Googe's preference for unadorned Protestant worship over the more elaborate rituals of the old faith. The narrative also devalues the role of the priest as an intermediary between divinity and man. Gregory's communication with God is direct and intimate, while the followers of Apollo are obliged to seek recourse to the priest for spiritual guidance. In the ongoing Reformation debate, reformers were anxious to diminish the clergy's standing in the church, pointing instead to the centrality of the Word. Here Googe, in presenting this tale to the Darrell sisters, offers an alternative view of religious service, expressed, one presumes, with the silent hope that they will come to reject the perceived constraints of the formalistic faith they have been born into. His use of Eusebius is highly selective, and ultimately sectarian, but is a further manifestation of the *Shippe*'s overall purpose, an evangelical concern to introduce the reader to reformed ideas, and to persuade the moral waverer into dedicated pious living.

Googe Plagiarized: Anthony Nixon's *The Christian Navy*

As we have seen, *The Shippe of Safegarde* seems to have attracted little notice in Googe's time. By 1602 it was so thoroughly forgotten that the pamphleteer Anthony Nixon could publish a slightly abbreviated verbatim plagiarism of the title poem as his own work under the title of *The Christian Navy*, brazenly dedicating it as a "worke of willing mind . . . begot by true affection" to the Archbishop of Canterbury, John Whitgift.[75] In this redaction Googe's work apparently enjoyed somewhat greater popularity, for it was reissued in 1605.[76] The success of this literary larceny apparent-

---

[73] See Rufinus, 2: 953–56.

[74] A full assessment of the historical St. Gregory is given in Robin Lane Fox, *Pagans and Christians* (Harmondsworth: Viking, 1986), 517–42.

[75] London: Simon Stafford, 1602.

[76] Early bibliographers frequently described *The Shippe of Safegarde* and *The Christian Navy*, but none seems to have observed that they are virtually identical. Nixon's plagiarism was noted in Pollard & Redgrave's *Short Title Catalogue*, 2nd ed., revised W. A. Jackson, F. S. Fer-

ly emboldened Nixon to continue the practice more subtly in some of his later writings.[77] One may hope, at least, that he endured a moment of discomfort as he copied out Googe's stern disapproval of those "Who faine would be esteemed cunning men, / While as they steale the fruits of others pen" (*Shippe*, st. 203; cf. *The Christian Navy*, G3^{v}).

To Nixon's credit, his rendition of the poem improves it in certain ways. Nixon omits Googe's front matter, of course, and the tales from Eusebius; he shortens the poem by cutting eleven stanzas and by shrinking the remaining stanzas from eight lines to seven; finally, he helps the reader by marking off the discussion of each vice or virtue with a horizontal rule and a large initial capital. Nixon usually just omits the sixth line of Googe's ottava rima stanza, rendering a seven-line iambic pentameter stanza rhyming *ababacc*. Often, however, it is more convenient for him to make different changes that yield a rhyme-royal stanza, rhyming *ababbcc*. Occasionally Nixon's condensations sacrifice something worthwhile, as when in stanza 6 he eliminates Googe's strong image, "With sayles full thwackt with winde and lustie showe," while leaving the rest of the stanza unchanged, or in stanza 9, where he loses Googe's description of the Christian sailor as "Nie drownd with cares, and bet [beaten] with miserie." Most often, however, the omitted material is excess verbiage, and Nixon's condensations improve the text. For example, Googe's lumbering lines in stanza 136, "With lothsome showe as stinking noysome weedes, / That freshest flower in gardens doth deface," become in Nixon's hands simply, "As noysome weeds the freshest flowres deface" (E2^{v}).

The thirty-three years between Googe's composition and Nixon's plagiarism saw changes in language and style that Nixon now and then troubles to reflect. Thus Googe's "never have no ende" (st. 43) becomes "never have an end" (B4); Googe's "If that the burden" (st. 50) becomes "And if the burden" (C1); and Googe's "Least that" (st. 79) becomes "For feare" (C4^{v}). Occasionally Nixon's revisions reflect an awareness of the more variable pentameter line that made the verse of Googe and his contemporaries sound rather wooden by 1590. Thus Googe's "Where you shall finde the fruites of all your gaine" (st. 43) becomes the slightly more supple "Finding at length the fruits of all your gayne" (B4). Similarly, Nixon sometimes eases the obsessive early Elizabethan alliteration, as when he changes Googe's "So doth this foule and filthie fonde desire" (st.

---

guson, and Katherine F. Pantzer (London: Bibliographical Society, 1986), 1: 530, and in Eccles, "Barnabe Googe in England, Spain, and Ireland," 362, n.48.

[77] See J. Payne Collier, *A Bibliographical and Critical Account of the Rarest Books in the English Language*, 4 vols. (New York: David G. Francis and Charles Scribner & Co., 1866), 3: 61–67; and also his *Poetical Decameron*, 2 vols. (Edinburgh: Archibald Constable & Co., 1820), 1: 302–3.

90) to "So doth this fond insatiate desire" (D2). Elsewhere, Nixon corrects Googe's hypermetrical lines and other errors, although he is guilty of errors of his own, such as a stanza with an unrhymed line (F4) or a misplaced heading (Fl^{v}, G1).

Despite these improvements, however, Nixon's version yields to Googe's original in important respects. Nixon omits entirely the most fully allegorized passage in "The Ship of safegarde," stanzas 110–19, where the errant Christian sailors, lured by Sirens, go ashore on the Island of Fleshly Pleasure and are led to a Circe-like Queen who turns them into animals or subjects them to the torments of a Petrarchan lover's hell. Nixon may have regarded this passage as objectionable in a book presented to Archbishop Whitgift, or simply as stylistically passé. He also usually avoids repeating Googe's uses of the word "devil" or the names of devils. By cutting it he bends the poem further from poetic allegory and more towards sermon, a process reinforced by several further instances in which he abandons Googe's ongoing nautical metaphor. On the other hand, Nixon does not flinch from Googe's firm Protestant insistence on the primacy of the scriptures (sts. 150–53; E4–E4^{v}). While it is to Googe's credit that over three decades after his poem was written it seemed to Nixon worth stealing for the Archbishop, one must regret that the plagiarist, even though he was writing after Spenser had shown the possibilities of allegorical narrative, did not attempt to develop more fully the rudimentary dark conceit that so fitfully animates Googe's poem.

TEXTUAL INTRODUCTION

A newe Booke called the Shippe of safegarde (STC 12049) exists in a single printing, of which three copies are known to scholars, one in the Folger Shakespeare Library, Washington, D.C., a photocopy of which with the kind permission of the library has served as our copytext, and identical copies in the Newberry Library, Chicago, and the John Rylands University Library in Manchester, England, which we have examined both in the original and, for detailed comparison and transcription, in photocopy or microfilm versions. No corrections appear to have been made during the printing process, for the printer's errors listed in our Textual Notes appear in all three copies. The title page from the Folger copy is reproduced on page iii and is discussed in McKerrow and Ferguson (101). It displays the title within a woodcut border. At the top appears the royal coat of arms, at the bottom that of the Stationers' Company, while William Seres's monogram is reproduced at either side. Seres had first used this title page design in 1567 for *The psalter, after the translation of the greate bible.* In the year of *The Shippe of safegarde,* Seres used the cut for two other publications: Sir John Cheke's *The hurt of sedition* and the anonymous *An annswere to the proclamation of the rebels in the north.* Eight years later the title page made its final appearance in E. Tilney's *A briefe discourse of duties in mariage;* clearly the cut had by this stage left Seres's workshop as this book was printed by Henry Denham. *The Shippe of safegarde* has no colophon. The collation and contents are as follows:

Collation: 8°, A4, B–E8, F4 [sigs. A2, 1–4 (B–E), F1 and F2 signed]. 40 leaves, unpaginated.

Contents: A1: title (verso blank); A2: "To hys verie good Sisters *Mistresse Phyllyp Darell,* and Mistresse Fraunces Darell, *of the house of Scotney*" (dedicatory epistle set in roman); A3v: "To the Reader" (introductory poem set in italic); on A4^{v} [rectangular tailpiece of vine-like pattern, 200 x 440 mm.]; B1: "The

Ship of safegarde" (poem set in black letter); E5: "The death of S. Polycarpus *Bishop of Smyrna,* and disciple to saint John. *Euseb.lib.4*" (poem set in black letter); F2^{v}: "A Priest of Apollo straunge-*ly converted.* Euseb.lib.4" (poem set in black letter). Running heads: "*The Epistle*" (large italic), A2^{v}–A3; "To the Reader" (large roman), A3^{v}–A4^{v}; "*The ship of safegard*" (large italic), B1^{v}–E4^{v}; "*Of the death*" and "*of S. Polycarpe*" (large italic) alternating verso-recto, E5^{v}–F2^{v}; "*Apollos Priest converted*" (large italic), F3–F4^{v}.

In reprinting Googe's poems written in fourteeners ("To the Reader" and "The death of S. Polycarpus"), we have followed the common practice of his time by dividing the long lines into half-lines of four and three feet. In transcribing the text we have modernized usage of *i/j, u/v,* and the long *s*, and we have expanded typographical abbreviations except for the ampersand. We have ignored swash letters, ornamental capitals, different type sizes, and all ligatures. A few other emendations that correct obvious misprints are listed in the Textual Notes. We have retained the system of punctuation used in the original, which is generally governed by the patterns of the verse rather than by syntax. Thus each line of the ottava rima stanzas in "The Ship of safegarde" almost invariably ends with a comma, even though no punctuation or a full stop may be required by the syntax. A similar but less regular practice marks off the half-lines and couplets of Googe's divided fourteeners in "To the Reader" and "The death of S. Polycarpus" and the endings of the pentameter lines of "A Priest of Apollo straungely converted." Stanza and line numbers have been added by the editors. Signature numbers in brackets precede the material to be found on the designated page of the copytext. Interpretations of difficult passages and other comments are provided in the Explanatory Notes, as are definitions of archaic terms on their first occurrences. The Glossary Index indicates in which notes such definitions are to be found. Full publication data for works cited in abbreviated form in the Explanatory Notes may be found in the list of works consulted.

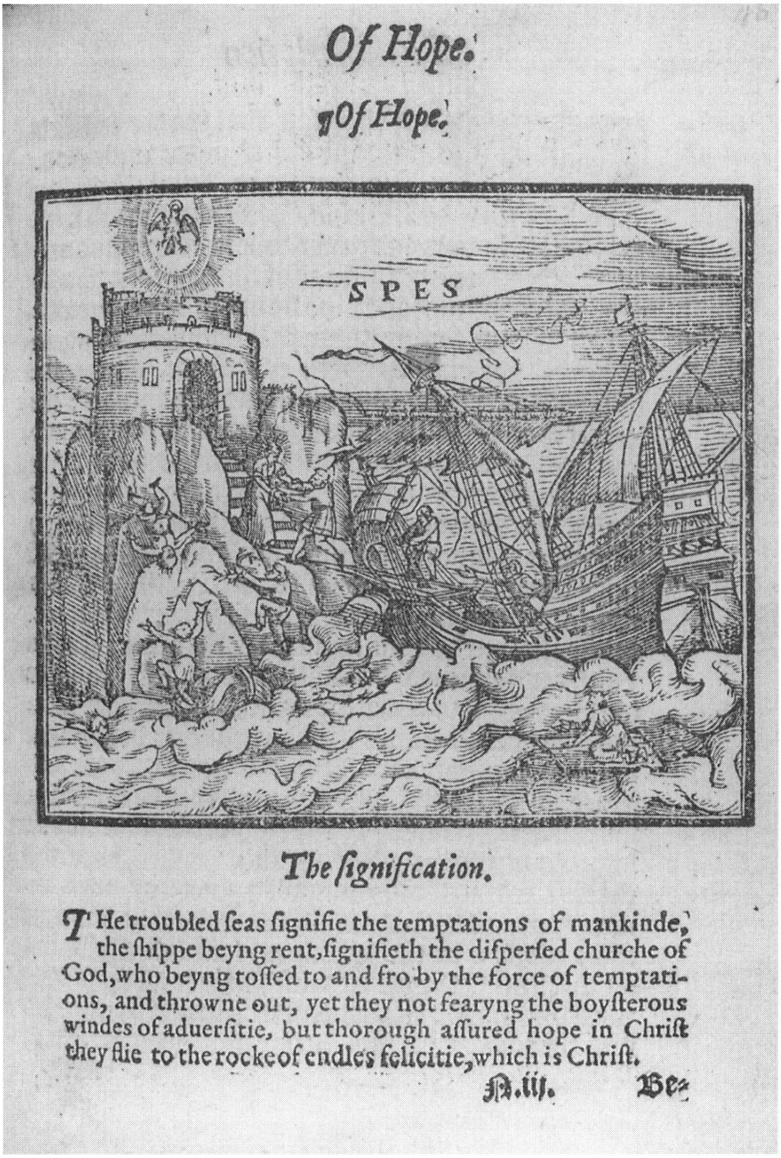

Of Hope.

¶*Of Hope.*

The ſignification.

THe troubled ſeas ſignifie the temptations of mankinde, the ſhippe beyng rent, ſignifieth the diſperſed churche of God, who beyng toſſed to and fro by the force of temptations, and throwne out, yet they not fearyng the boyſterous windes of aduerſitie, but thorough aſſured hope in Chriſt they flie to the rocke of endles felicitie, which is Chriſt.

N.iii. Be-

Plate II

Allegorical woodcut illustrating "Hope," from Stephen Bateman's *A christall glasse of christian reformation* (London: John Day, 1569), N3.
Shelfmark C.37.d.2.

A newe Booke

called the Shippe

of safegarde,

wrytten by

G.B.

Anno.1569.

Imprinted at Lon
don by W. Seres.

¶ To hys verie good Sisters *Mistresse Phillyp Darell,* and Mistresse Fraunces Darell, *of the house of Scotney*

OFTEN WITH MY SELFE considering (my nowne good Sisters) your vertuous and well disposed minds, in these your yong and tender yeares, I thought it meete (as well to shewe my good will towards you, as to satisfie your well inclined affections) to take some travaile in finding out such matter, as neither I might accompt my time vainly spent in wryting, nor you yours evill employed in reading. Debating thus a whyle with my selfe what matter myght best herein serve both our turnes, I was thorowly resolved with asmuch diligence as I could to make some discourse upon the perfite estate of a true christian, an estate above all others most happie and worthy, if it were as well renowmed for lyfe, as it is reverent for name, and perceyving the lyves of Christians in these dayes so farre differing from the sinceritie that is required in a Christian professour, I gave for tytle to my Booke the counterfeyt Christian, wherein I [A2v] declared the great disorders of this our tyme, as also the wonderfull vertues and puritie of lyfe, that gloriously shyned among the first and auncyent professours of Christ, whiche Booke beyng encreased to some largenesse of volume, and even almost readie to be publyshed under the patronage and protection of your two names, by yll favourd misfortune perished. Wherwithal somthing discontented that both I should thus bee defrawded of the effect of my long travayle, and you of that which so long and so earnestly I ment you. With a scarse quiet mind I hastily began this volume, which (bicause of the daungers of this worlde, whereby the soule enclosed in the barke of sinfull fleshe wyth great hasard passeth) I named the Ship of safegarde, a Ship but rudely furnished, and God knowes symply rygged, as the great haste and small tyme enforced, wanting both strength of tymber and comlynesse of proporcion, two evydent signes of an unskilfull workeman. Notwithstanding howsoever it be, I dedicate it unto you as an earnest token of my good wyll towardes you, not doubting but you will so accept it, wherunto I had also thought to have added (bicause I know you delight in stories) [A3] the lyves and actes of dyvers men in the primative Church, whereof I began with one or two, but bicause they were tedious, and my leisure but little, I left them and proceeded no farther. God poure upon you his plenteous blessyng, graunt you long and prosperous yeres on earth, and after your passage from this vale of wretchednesse, everlasting rest and joy in the kingdome of Heaven. From London the fourtenth of Februarie.

Your louing brother in lawe. G.B.

[A3v]

To the Reader.

WHo seekes to treade that happie path,
that leades to perfite blisse:
And faine would finde the certayne way,
that many wandring misse.
Must banish ease and bend himselfe,
to abyde both care and paine:
And seeke to conquer eche delight,
and worldly pleasure vaine.
For as the way but narrow is,
that leadeth straight to joy:
So is it all beset with thornes,
and briers that anoy.
In evrie place are stubbles and prickes,
that stayes the feeble Feete:
And lothsome for the time it seemes,
that after prooves most sweete.
A fearefull hart refuseth quite,
to walke that painefull way:
But carefull mindes regarde not paine,
such pleasure to assay.
Both wayes before the eyes doth lye,
and view of evrie braine,
The tone both narrow sowre and sharpe,
the other smooth and plaine.
The tone doth after smart and griefe,
bring men where God doth raine:
[A4] The other after pleasures sweete,
bringes everlasting paine:
The tone doth glister in the eyes,
with faire and pleasant ground.
The other lothsome seemes and darke,
and scarcely to be found.
But hardest thinges experience tries,
are often found most sweete:

And high attempts for valiant hartes,
are thought of all most meete.
Thou therefore that doest minde to see:
the joyes celestiall:
And to beholde that happie face,
that never perishe shall
Forsake this waye that pleasant is,
at first unto the eye:
And as a daunger foule and great,
such flattring pleasures flye.
Tread thou the path that mounteth up,
to place where God doth live:
And doth for everie paine on earth,
a thousand pleasures give.
Such pleasures as doe farre surmount,
the fading pleasures here:
As farre as doth the Sunne excell,
the Moone in shyning clere.
Faynt not for anye griefe or paine,
nor never wearie be:
[A4v] Well may the way be passed, and God
himselfe shall succour thee.
For God doth ayde all those that give
themselves with all their might,
To finde his wayes and courage gives
to all that well doe fight.
Against the flattrings of the worlde,
and fansies vaine of minde,
No better Capitaine canst thou have,
nor guide of better kinde.

[B1]

The Ship of safegarde

(1)
THe wandring wight that in the raging seas
Wyth sayling Barke doth seke the happy port,
No leysure hath to give himselfe to ease:
Ne time he findes wherein to play or sport.
Eche long delay, eche calme doth him displease,
Hym listeth not to lynger in such sort,
In nothing joyes, in nothing pleasure findes,
Save in the blastes of prosperous happie windes.

(2)
His carefull braine is busied evermore,
In vewyng well his Compasse and his Carde
And minding still what daungers lye before,
What swelling sands, what rocks, what Havens barde
Wyth skilfull head he seekes the safest shore,
And thetherwarde doth sayle with good regarde,
Brings home his Bark through storms & tempests great
To happie port and long desired seat.

(3)
The unskilfull head, and rechelesse ydle minde,
Contrariewise doth give himselfe to rest,
Not fearing stormes nor boystrous blasts of winde,
But in the middest of daungers feareth least
And thinkes the Haven happily to finde,
When stormes are past, and tempests cleerely ceast,
Thus guyded evill his shyp on rocks doth fall,
And castes awaye both frayght and foole and all.

(4)
Even so the will and fansie vayne of man,
That through this worlde his painefull passage makes,
Who ought to seeke by all the meanes he can

Through daungers deepe, and lothsome lowring lakes,
That happie port for which his course began,
For which eche carefull minde his travaile takes,
In thousand harmes and thousand daungers prest,
Doth give himselfe to careless ease and rest,

[B1^{v}] (5)
Regarding not the hasard of himselfe,
Nor taking heede his fleshly foyst to guide,
Full fraught with sin, and care of worldly pelfe,
Makes no account of wether, winde or tide,
But blindly strikes himselfe on everie shelfe,
And in the flouds of mischiefe wanders wide,
Till on the rocks he desperately doth light,
And loseth all for lacke of guiding right.

(6)
Within the seas of fonde affection blinde,
That through the world in everie place doth flowe,
Sayles everie Wight that liveth here by kinde,
And runnes the race that fancie forth doth blowe,
And kepes the course that pleaseth best his minde,
With sayles full thwackt with winde and lustie showe,
But of ten thousand that thus doe bravely fleete,
Scarse ten at length doe with the Haven meete.

(7)
The Haven faire I meane of perfite joye,
Where chiefest pleasure hath hir biding place,
Where joye surmounts, where griefe can not anoye,
Where lives the king of everlasting grace,
That well rewardes eche minde that doth employe
Them selfe in travaile to attaine that place:
And doth condemne to everlasting paine,
All those that him forsake for pleasures vaine.

(8)
The seas be rough, the passage full of paine,
The daungers great, the journey large and long,
The Pilots yll, the Coast is nothing plaine,
The force but weake, the enimies stout and strong,
The lets a number that labour to detaine,
And flattring showes that leades the maister wrong,

The streites of Marrocke are not halfe so yll,
Ne race of Britaine, ne Charybdis, nor Scyll,

[B2] (9)
Wherefore in vaine we strive without a guide,
To passe these seas where thousand daungers bee,
With rocks and shelves beset on everie side,
Where nought but death the fearefull eye can see,
Now forced with windes, now driven backe with tide,
Nie drownd with cares, and bet with miserie,
Amased with mists, and wandring without light,
Except we finde the helpe of holy sprite.

(10)
Which spirite that in our journey we may have,
With humble hart and earnest prayer made,
With knees bowed downe, his ayde here let us crave,
That he vouchsafe to teach us plaine the trade
Of sayling right, and from all daungers save
Our simple soules, that through these seas must wade,
With stedfast fayth to him thus let us pray,
That he may guide us through this doubtfull way.

(11)
O sacred spirite that all things well doest guide,
And bringest eche good thought to his desire,
And sufferest not no error to abide,
Whereas it likes thy grace for to inspire:
That doest for every humble hart provide,
And shewest the way with thy celestiall fire,
Powre downe thy grace, direct my feeble hand,
That I may shew where perfite blisse doth stand.

(12)
By thee we may be sure the way to finde,
That leadeth straight to perfite joy and blisse,
By thee we shunne the rocks and daungers blinde,
That makes us oft the Haven faire to misse,
Thou onlye art the starre that guidest the minde
Unto the place where perfite pleasure is.
Give me thy light, cast downe thy beames from hie,
That I may show which way the course doth lie.

[B2v] (13)
The wretched seas of worldly pleasures vaine,
The mischiefes and the harmes that comes thereby,
The flattering showes, that trouble most the brayne,
The noysome lusts, and fancies there that lie,
That causers are of everlasting paine,
And casts away the soules that travaile by:
I will declare, and eke which way to runne,
What course to keepe, what daungers for to shunne.

(14)
Within these seas, when first we enter in,
When first to winde our sayles committed bee,
When pleasantly on calmed streames we swim,
A mightie rocke lo streight at hand we see
Of massie Gold, all decked and garnisht trim,
That doth allure the eye of eche degree,
The compasse great with corners out doth lie,
The heigth whereof doth reach the starrie skie.

(15)
A stately rocke beset with Diamondes faire,
And pouldred round about with Rubies red,
Where Emralds greene doo glister in the aire,
With Mantell blew of Saphyres over spred:
Where wants no stone that nature can repaire,
No pearle of price nor Jewell polished.
Another heaven for the time it seemes,
And oft for heaven foolish men it deemes.

(16)
With swelling sands it lies encompast round,
And many a ragged reach it sendeth out,
Whereby full many a thousand have bene drownd,
Yet never cease they for to saile about,
In gasing still upon this gorgeous ground,
Approching neerer not having any doubt,
Till on the sands with hastie course they slide,
And lose themselves upon this piere of pride,

[B3] (17)
No greater daunger shalt thou lightly finde,
That more mishap and mischiefe more doth make,

Than this, that pluckes away the saylers minde,
And causeth him contrarie course to take.
Who forward puft with fonde vainglorious winde,
His perfite way doth utterly forsake,
Till on the sands his Keale here happes to knocke,
And dasheth all a sunder on this rocke.

(18)
A wretched rocke that mounting to the skie,
(Contenting not himselfe with earthly spoyle)
Once overthrew the Angels sitting hie,
And cast them headlong from their happy soyle
To darkest place where wayling now they lie,
With griefe ashamed of so great a foyle.
The chiefe estates and princes here below,
Have eke good cause this daungerous place to know.

(19)
The raging waves doth belching upward cast
The wretched wrackes that round about doe fleete,
The silken sayles and glistering golden Mast,
Lies all to torne and troden under feete.
The witlesse throng of women swarming fast,
Like Parrats pied in garments farre unmeete,
With scarfes and fethers like to souldiers drest,
With painted heare and shamelesse bared brest.

(20)
A monstrous sort of men there shalt thou see,
Not men, but devils sure that beare the face
Of men, that never can contented bee
With comly garments meete, but (voyde of grace)
Forgetting quite their auncient olde degree,
To women chaunged, their manly shapes deface
With slender wastes, as Maydens most doe use.
And frisled heare like harlots of the stewes.

[B3v] (21)
With countnance coy, and forhead forced hie,
And staring top as lately frayed with sprites,
In rich attire, to feede the gasers eie,
That evermore in glistring show delights,
A sort of beasts, whose chiefest joy doth lie,

In decking up themselves for wondring sights,
In yelow, red, and Purple to be seene,
Sometimes like fooles in gownes of gawdy greene.

(22)
As painted tombes that stinch and filth containe,
And Arras faire that rotten wals doth hide,
So doe these fooles, with all their garments vaine,
And fresh attire drest up in pompe and pride,
Nought else but beastly mindes and doltish braine,
Faire covered, keepe which filthie else were spide,
For underneath their garments glistering brave,
Lies mindes corrupt as rotten bones in grave.

(23)
A sinfull sort that wholy spend their life,
In setting out their stinking carcasse here,
Who night and daye doe passe with care and strife,
In studying how they fairest may appeare,
And wearie soone of fashions olde and rife,
Disguise themselves in newe disguised geare,
As not consisting of their proper minde,
But chaunging still as chaunged things they finde.

(24)
Flie thou this rocke and take good heede thereto,
For who so keepes this dreadfull daungerous way,
Shall run the race that him shall quite undo,
And misse the marke by sayling thus astray,
That should him bring the happie Haven to,
No mischiefe more doth breede the soules decay,
No greater harme can hap to mortall kinde,
Than for to run upon this daunger blinde.

[B4] (25)
For who so once upon the same doth fall,
Forgetteth God, forgets his owne estate,
Of good or vertue makes no count at all,
So he may live aloft without a mate,
And for to attaine a little glorie small,
He nought esteemes of mightie Jove the hate,
Who of all other sorts can worst abide,
Such kinde of men as most delights in pride,

(26)
But to avoyde this rocke and hasard great,
Strike thou thy sayles and beare thy countnance low,
Shun sumptuous shew, regard not Lordly seat,
Nor to be knowne, seeke rather God to know,
Who being Lord and prince of glory great,
Came downe from hie, and lived on earth below
In poore attire and simple show beside,
To teache us men for to beware of pride.

(27)
Remember still how that the loftie minde
That in this world doth seeke to glister so,
Blowne on this rocke by fonde vainglorious winde,
Fall headlong downe to everlasting wo,
Where no release of torments shall he finde,
But as he wont in colours bright to go,
So bright in flames of fires shall he blase,
Who flamed afore for everie eye to gase.

(28)
Be never prowde of what so nature gives,
For what she gives, in time she takes away,
The fairest creature, the finest wit that lives,
In shortest time we see doth cleane decay,
Away goeth all though never so sore it grieves,
No pleasant thing can here have longer stay,
What follie then is it to set delight,
On fading smokes, and lose the heavens bright?

[B4v] (29)
Be lowly minded, of meeke and humble cheare,
Thinke glory unmeete for men of base degree,
Since God for pride with Angels would not beare,
Be well assured he will not beare it in thee,
To late thou shalt repent, when thou shalt see,
The sober sort most simply clothed heare
With glistring robes amongst the Angels hie,
And thou thy selfe with Devils low to lie,

(30)
The griefe beside is great of troubled minde,
That in this world they often time sustaine:

As want of wealth that stops their fancies blinde,
Whereby they fare like Tantalus in paine,
In everie place men costly clad they finde,
And they themselves can not thereto attaine,
Sometime diseases sore doth them deface,
Then farewell joy a ground is all their grace.

(31)
The Christall Glasse wherein they wont to prie
With joyfull hart, to see their beautie cleare,
Gives out a shape unpleasant to the eie,
Whereas their crabbed countnaunce doth appeare,
All fret with holes, where Pockes of late did lie,
Downe falles the visage then with heavie cheare,
And mourning tho, from thence apace they goe,
As men amased with some sodeine woe.

(32)
The pleasant fame for ever now is gone,
That wonted was their eares for to delight,
O marke him well, lo yender goeth one
In whom hath Nature sought to shew hir might,
A comlier creature you can not looke uppon,
Of better favour or framed in better plight,
Now no such sounde but scornde on evrie side,
While eche one sayth beholde the ende of pride.

[B5] (33)
Therfore take heede that in these seas dost sayle,
Let not this vaine delight deceive thy minde,
But rather strive against it to prevayle,
And seeke the chanell of lowlynesse to finde,
Which when thou gettest, no tempest can thee quayle,
Thou needest not feare no storme nor chaunging winde,
For there is harbrow safe for evrie Wight,
That in this happy Chanell haps to light.

(34)
This daunger past, and left aloofe behinde,
Before thine eyes doth straight againe appeare,
A fowle deformed pile and hasard blinde,
That castes awaye all such as travaile neare,
A lothsome rocke and hurtfull to the minde,

All overgrowne with mosse and rustie geare,
Deformed to the eye, yet doth allure
Of earthly men the earthy mindes unpure.

(35)
A daungerous place that numbers doth destroy,
Of such as carelesse are of sayling right,
Whose brutish mindes have here no other joy,
Then on the drosse of earth to set delight,
This mischiefe great doth basest mindes anoy,
And never hurts the hawtie heavenly sprite,
But greedy mindes and such as are not wise,
This lothsome place is called Avarice.

(36)
A number great of wrackes here shalt thou see,
That thicke in thousands about this place doe swarme,
That never could alive admonishde bee
For to beware of this so great a harme,
Nor to eschew this present jeoperdie,
Suffysed no words their Gracelesse mindes to charme,
Nor no advise could cause them sayle aright,
Till on this rocke they wilfully doe light.

[B5v] (37)
With countnance pale and wan thou shalt beholde
Their carcasse quite consumed unto nought,
Their wearish limmes with cares congealed colde,
Their bloud dried up with sorow and with thought,
Their feeble fingars still clasping in of golde.
Desire whereof to them this mischiefe brought,
Hanged round about with bags on everie side,
The poyse whereof doth cause them there to bide.

(38)
Upon the sands great Caskets heaped lie,
And Cofers stuft with everie kinde of coyne,
Scraped up by fraude and filthy usurie,
Now here, now there, wheresoever they could purloyne,
By force, by fraude, or any villanie,
Of rich, of poore, of Courtier or of Cloyne,
They wey not where nor how they doe it get,
For all is fish with them that comes to net.

(39)
A filthie minde that travailes to no ende,
But for to please the still desiring eye,
Esteemes no paine, regardes no foe nor frende,
Helpes not himselfe, nor no man else thereby,
In sparing, joyes, and pineth if he spende,
Is never good untill the time he die,
Which time he pleasures many with his hoord,
As doth the Swine when as he comes to boord,

(40)
A brutish sort that never can rejoyce
Whyle here they live, for carke, for feare or toyle,
Still dreaming that they heare the dreadfull voyce
Of thiefe at hand, or souldier them to spoyle,
Or sodeine death that makes of them no choyse,
But takes them hence amid their most turmoyle,
And rakes them up in earth enclosed deepe,
Where voyde of gaine and kept for paine they sleepe.

[B6] (41)
What profites them their heapes of riches great,
For which alive they tooke such care and paine,
Oft wanting sleepe, forbearing often meat,
With greedie minde to encrease their treasure vaine,
When lothsome wormes their carcasse vile shall eat,
And Fiendes convay their soules to Plutoes raigne,
Rung downe to hell with Cursings of the poore,
Whose wives and children lie weeping without doore.

(42)
What helpes the welth that doth not serve the neede?
What good doth Golde that doth but feede the eie?
What gaine but griefe have they for all their neede?
That labour here for money till they die,
Which long kept in is spent at length with speede,
Perhaps of him that was the enimie,
A goodly thing to pine for riches so,
And know not who shall have them when we go.

(43)
O wretched beasts, that never have no ende,
Of this your vile and covetous desire,

Why spare you thus that other folkes shall spende?
You toyle and moyle like Bayard in the mire,
Your selves to grave before your time you sende,
And so from thence to everlasting fire,
Where you shall finde the fruites of all your gaine,
In broyling flames and never ceassing paine.

(44)
The poore opprest whom in this world you polde,
Your selves shall see to glister in the skie,
And call and ball to them for water colde,
To coole your heate in torments where you lie,
But all in vaine, for this you have bene tolde,
By him that preached with Lasarus from hie,
And since you would not by others harmes take heede,
Blame no man tho in like sort if you speede.

[B6v] (45)
God hath himselfe declared to you before,
That even as slow rich men to heaven flie,
And enter in as hardly at the dore,
As doth the Camell passe a Needles eie.
Your burden great extorted from the poore,
Doth keepe you downe, you can not mount so hie,
The path is narrow, the gates are very straight,
You can not enter, with so great a waight.

(46)
Your factors lie not there to aunswere you,
Your bill of debt, nor no such other geare,
Nor by exchaunge you can have nothing due,
Your double usance is but single there,
The trade is chaunged, the world is altered new,
Your toyle for gaine shall purchace homely cheare,
Your ten in hundreds will scarcely then amount,
When for your dealings you shall be callde to count.

(47)
A thousand actions shalbe entred there,
Against you for your fraude and usurie,
And Lawyer none shall shew his face for feare,
Though you retaine him with his double fee,
Least that in pleading it plainly doth appeare,

His Clients cause and his for to agree,
The Judge is wise, and easly can espie
If fault or fraude doe under colours lie.

(48)
With quaking hart at barre then shalt thou stande,
Without advice or any other aide,
Hie holding up thy giltie gilted hande,
For feare of sentence utterly dismaide.
Thy whole accompt shall throughly there be scande,
And everie title perfitely be wayde.
And everie pennie how it hath bene spent,
That unto thee for purpose good was lent.

[B7] (49)
Therfore who sayleth nere this lothsome place,
Fall off betimes and keepe another way,
Have in thy minde the Haven faire of grace,
And from thy Compasse go not much astray.
Beholde thy Carde and keepe a perfite race,
And in such daungers make no long delay,
No ancours here beware that thou doe cast,
For ship and all will soone be layde up fast.

(50)
If that the burden that thou bearst be great,
Cast over borde both bags and baggage quite,
Let never Golde thee of thy joy defeat,
Safe shalt thou sayle and better travaile light,
Than overladen to lose the happie seate,
And never finde the gorgeous Haven bright,
Of rest and blisse, where free and frankest mindes
Doe shrowde their ships escapde from greedy windes.

(51)
Well mayst thou employe the riches here thou hast,
And please the king and Lorde of glorie hie,
If that thou makst of them no wanton wast,
Ne scrapest them up in Coffers close to lie,
But layst them where they may be safest plast,
Upon the poore that live in miserie,
And upon such as comfortlesse remaine,
This is the best and surest kinde of gaine.

(52)
How goodly a thing is it for to relieve
Thafflicted case of men with neede opprest,
Whom daily cares and troubled minde doth grieve,
That scarse can finde an houre of quiet rest,
Whilst thou hast thousands hanging on thy sleeve,
And spendst thy dayes with welth and pleasure blest,
Remember well, that richesse are but lent,
And nothing ours but that which well is spent.

[B7v] (53)
Another mischiefe in the waye doth stand,
With ougly shape and vile deformed sight,
Encompast round with quicke and quivering sand,
That swallowes up all such as thereon light,
Foule swarmes of serpents crawle on everie hand,
With gastly teeth and stings embrued with spite,
Whose hissing tongues doe yelde a filthie noyse,
A lothsome sound, a most unpleasant voyce.

(54)
About this rocke in everie place they crall,
And shake their tongues at them that travaile by,
Whom envious windes doth cause with them to fall,
And spite compelles to run their course awrie,
Most wretched guides to guide a Barke withall,
And most unmeete such daungerous seas to trie,
Who never ceasse till all be overthrowne,
Till Foyst and fraight be under surges blowne.

(55)
Here poysned vapors continually doe rise,
And yelling noyse and hatefull crie is hard,
The hellish cloudes so dase the saylers eies,
That scarce he sees his Compasse or his Card,
Except he skilfull be and verie wise,
And of his course have alwayes good regard,
And cast about to meete some better winde,
That may him bring unto his port assignde.

(56)
The tide is strong that runneth thereabout,
The weather great that beates upon the cost,

The holde to weake to thinke to rid it out,
Whereby full many at ancour have been lost,
That thought it safe and made therof no dout,
And perished where as they trusted most,
This harmfull place Detraction hath to name,
An auncient enmy to the Barke of fame.

[B8] (57)
Upon this rocke as lost and cast awaye,
All those whose tongues delight in yll report,
And make of slaunders but a kinde of playe,
Wherewith themselves most spitefully they sport,
Defacing quite by all the meanes they maye
Both name and fame of everie kinde of sort,
Still charging them with this thing and with that,
And oftentimes they wote not well with what.

(58)
Of everie man their tongue must run at large,
Nought can be sayde but must their judgement passe,
Their oares must be a board in everie barge,
With eche mans life they mell, and yet (alasse)
Their owne is worst, whereof they take no charge,
Their owne deformities they view not in the glasse,
But looke in others what they finde amisse,
Apace at that with hatefull tongue they hisse.

(59)
Whatsoever they see, or whatsoever they heare,
They make much worse than it was sayde or ment,
Their cancred tongues so spitefull doe appeare,
That still to yll they chaunge the good intent,
And make it darke that of it selfe was cleare,
Bicause it doth not their momish mindes content,
What likes them not must streight dispraised bee,
Their eyes be dim, they can no vertue see.

(60)
The vertuoust man that can be found alyve,
Can not escape their spitefull poysned tong,
Though that by all the meanes he can, he strive,
With vertuous life to cease the rumor sprong,
No vertuous act these Waspes away can drive,

But Harpy like they file all with their dung,
On everie table, on everie place they laye
Their filth and stinch, and all things foule araye.

[B8v] (61)
Most lothsome fowles that have no other food,
But feede upon the fame of evrie man,
A filthie race, a cursed beastly brood,
Who while themselves no kinde of vertue can,
Yet in their fond and franticke furious mood,
They others spoyle of vertuous fame, and whan
They see that any seeke to live upright,
Their envious harts are like to breake with spite.

(62)
This wretched sort have swarmed evermore,
And have continued since the world was made,
Encreasing still with poyson kept in store,
Have never ceased their former cursed trade.
The godliest men in ages here before,
Could never cause this gracelesse sort to fade,
Doe what they could, they could not scape the sting
Of slaunderous tongues that more and more did spring.

(63)
Good Moyses olde, whose meeke and vertuous sprite,
Deserved well of evrie kinde of man,
Redressing wrong and alwayes furthring right,
Of whom a fame through all the world out ran,
In whom thalmightie Lord tooke great delight,
And patterne first of princely power began,
Could not escape this cancred currish sort,
That steyned his fame with lewde and ill report.

(64)
Reporting that he wrought by sorcerie,
Such wonders great as at that time they sawe,
And that he governde all by tyrannie,
Misusing men without all right or lawe,
Oppressing poore men with extremitie,
And better so to keepe them under awe,
Invented eke a fond religion vaine,
Devised only by his suttle braine.

[C1] (65)
The righteous Job that perfite was and just,
In whom the devill himselfe no fault could finde,
That served God with earnest faith and trust,
Obedient alwayes to his sacred minde,
Despised the world, despised all fleshly lust,
And never yeelded to affection blinde,
Yet felt the tongue and sting of slaunderous fame,
That found in him things worthy still of blame.

(66)
The holye prophetes that lived long agoe,
Like Gods on earth with vertue shining bright,
Who planted vertue where vice before did floe,
And on the heavens set their whole delight,
In teaching men the right way here to goe,
Were oft revilde with great reproche and spite,
And counted were seditious men and nought,
And such as all things out of order brought.

(67)
That happy messenger that brought the tidings glad,
That made the heavie hart for to rejoyce,
And cast away their dolefull countnance sad,
Revived with his healthfull heavenly voyce,
While as he preached with skinnes of Camell clad,
And brought them there of heaven happie choyse,
This cursed sort that all things wrong doe wrest,
Reporteth that the devill him possest.

(68)
The almightie Lord that downe from heaven hie,
Amongst us came to save such as were lost,
In whome no sinne nor kinde of vice did lie,
All full of grace and of the holy ghost,
Relieved all that unto him did crie,
And healed the sicke and sore in everie cost,
For all his vertue, for all his state devine,
Was called a glutton, a drinker deepe in wine.

[C1v] (69)
What should I call to minde the lewde report,
His good disciples gat for all their paine,

The infamies that toucht that sacred sort,
That gave their lives to encrease the heavenly raigne,
Who made of cruell torments but a sport,
And laught to scorne the Heathenish follies vaine,
The slaundrous tongues yet blased in everie place,
How they ne had religion, God, nor grace.

(70)
What should I tell the cancred carlish spite
Shewed openly at this same present daye,
Of such as boast in Gods behalfe to write,
Whose divelish tongues their hellish harts bewraye,
With blasphemies the heavens hie they smite,
And open mouthed with Wolvish voyce they braye,
Christ never taught no such uncourteous stile,
Ne seemes a Christian such lothsome language vile.

(71)
His sprite was meeke, his talke was alwayes milde,
With wordes of comfort evermore he spake,
All bitter speach from him was quite exilde,
Wherefore he bad all his example take,
And therefore he that thinks to be the childe
Of God, yll tongue must utterly forsake,
Uncourteous speach, of heaven doth not smell,
Nay rather stinketh of the pit of hell.

(72)
The Fiends that low beneath in Limbo lie,
Condemned to perpetuall paine and shame,
This churlish speach doe use continuallie,
And barke and baule at everie vertuous name,
Their hellish throtes with hatefull noyse doe crie,
And still accuse the saintes of God with blame,
Malebouche their maister doth them ever teache,
With cursed speach and poysned tongue to preache.

[C2] (73)
For slaunder there is counted vertue great,
In hatefull words they most of all delight,
Foule Infamie hath there the chiefest seate,
Acompanied with malice and with spite,
Who drops of envie continually doe sweate,

With hatefull show and foule ylfavored sight,
Repining still at all men that doe well,
And fearing God, doe shun the pit of hell.

(74)
But thou that seekest the happie heavenly seate,
Keepe not this course but well therof beware,
With spitefull tongue doe thou no man intreate,
Of others faults have never to much care,
But of thine owne that livest in daungers great,
Such toyle is much and well thou mayst it spare,
Of others faults what needst thou babble so,
When thou thy selfe hast vices many mo.

(75)
Let no mans life by thee defaced bee,
Take not awaye that thou canst not restore,
And looke what faults in others thou doest see,
Take heede that in thy selfe it be not more,
Report not yll, speake well of eche degree,
Encrease not griefe, but rather salve the sore,
Good woordes of all men gayneth laude and prayse,
Where as yll tongues are counted castawayes.

(76)
The gentle minde doth plainly represent,
A lively forme of God himselfe on hie,
Whose gracious will to goodnesse alwayes bent,
Delightes in myldenesse and in clemencie,
Who chiefly framed man for that intent,
To beare some showe of sacred majestie,
But cursed speach this picture out doth race,
And setteth up the devill in the place.

[C2v] (77)
Avoyde this daunger, and further from it flie,
Let not such mischiefe thy destruction bee,
For feare of losing all, sayle not to nie,
The losse is great, some safer shore goe see,
Where as at ancor thou mayst safely lie,
And rest, least to much travaile wearie thee,
In daungers great we may not run at length,
But rest a while to gather farther strength.

(78)
Hoyse up thy sayles, and give them to the winde,
These daungers past, the fewer do remaine,
Take courage good, and shew thy valiant minde,
And wey that pleasure followes after paine,
As after troubles quiet rest we finde,
That farre surmounts our toyles and travailes vaine,
For who so shrinkes with painfull things to meete,
Is farre unworthy for to taste the sweete.

(79)
Sayle on thy course, and cast a carefull eie,
About thy selfe within these seas so tost,
And ever marke what perils nere doe lie,
Least that thy negligence thee dearly cost,
And sounding sure, the hurtfull places trie,
Upon the which have thousand soules bene lost,
That carelesly with unadvised minde,
Have blindly folowed every puft of winde.

(80)
Before thy face at hand thou shalt beholde,
A foule great flat most lothsome for to see,
All overspred with limmes and bodies colde,
And Barkes and Boates that all to broken bee,
From whence the fraight upon the sands are rolde
And tumbled out thereon, both he and shee,
That sprawling lie upon this wretched place
With piteous looke and miserable face.

[C3] (81)
About the broken Barkes doe scattred lie,
Great tunnes of wine, of every kinde of sort,
And sumptuous tables with dishes heaped hie,
And costly bankets painted with disport,
The more to please the greedie gluttons eie,
That unto them oft useth to resort,
No kinde of flesh or fish there can be got,
But may be seene heaped up upon this plot.

(82)
All ready drest and furnisht to the eie,
With sundrie sauces the stomacke to allure,

Great platters there with wilde fowle full doe lie,
And spits full charged, that scarce their weight endure
Of deintie beasts and deintie birdes them bie,
As greedy lust can for the paunch procure,
Ech dish drest up as best may please the taste,
With great expence and small account of waste.

(83)
About these dishes round attending stand,
Ech vile disease that may be named or found,
The groning gowte with shackled foote and hand,
That scarse can staye from falling to the ground,
The Dropsie pale stands shaking on the sand,
With bellie swolne that yeeldes a hollowe sound,
The Fever hote sittes gaping here for winde,
Whose scorched tongue no taste in meate can finde.

(84)
Quotidians there and Quartans shalt thou see,
Now quaking colde, now burning all on flame,
There double, halfe, and bastard Tertians bee,
Continuars and those that Hecticke have to name,
With many more of this fraternitie,
Whereat Phisitions oft make pleasant game,
Attaining unto treasure and to welth,
More weying golde than any pacients helth.

[C3^{v}] (85)
A number great of sicknesses beside,
With piteous face and miserable show
May everie where about this place be spide,
That in these full fed fooles doe often grow,
As Pleuresies with torments in the side,
And jaundises in moving faint and slow,
With falling sicknesse that foming foule doth lie,
And Apoplexies murdring sodeinlie.

(86)
Most grievous paines and swimming in the head,
With Letharges forgetting everie thing,
And strangling quinsies with flaming humors fed,
That many men unto their graves doe bring,
Consuming Ptisicks long lingring in the bed,

And painfull Colicks whose griefe the guts do wring,
Both Stone & Strangurie lie here with grievous pain,
And many more that to rehearse were vain.

(87)
This fearefull place is called Gluttonie,
Wherein great numbers have bene cast awaye,
While as with greedie lust they sayled bie
And ran their course by negligence astraye,
Shun thou this daunger, and from this mischiefe flie,
And let not such an yll be thy decaye,
Let thousands dying there before thy face,
Example be for thee to shun this place.

(88)
A wretched vice, a sinfull crime it is,
To pamper up the flesh with his delight,
Whereby more prone it is to live amisse,
And more meete for to resist the sprite,
That Creature never seekes the place of blisse,
Nor never thinkes upon the heavens bright,
That studies here his greedie lust to please,
And for to passe his time in rest and ease.

[C4] (89)
The flesh will never here subdued bee,
Nor made obedient to the heavenly minde,
While as we farce it up in this degree,
With meate of everie daintie sort and kinde,
These fine fed folkes as daily we may see,
Are bent to lust and fleshly affections blinde,
But few of them that vertuous are or chast,
That have their guts thus inwardly bumbast.

(90)
As wood heaped up a hie upon the fire,
Or oyle cast in doth more augment the heate,
So doth this foule and filthie fonde desire
Of surfetting and cramming in of meate,
Encrease the flame of lecherous desire,
And makes the bodie blase with vices great,
Unmeete to follow any vertue good,
While as it is so cherished with foode.

(91)
The feeble braine with stinking vapors dased
That boyling in the stomacke upward rise,
Astonished and utterly amased,
Cannot aspire unto the hautie skies,
So weake it is, and so with surfets crased,
That in the body all a sleepe it lies,
Applying not it selfe the way to finde,
For to restraine the affections of the minde.

(92)
O what a sort may at this day be found,
That only give themselves to eate and drinke
Like brutish beasts, that grasing on the ground
Continually, of nothing else doe thinke,
What greater shame to Christians can redound?
What more before the face of God doth stinke?
Than thus to feede the paunch continually,
That to the soule is such an enimy.

[C4v] (93)
What folly greater can committed bee,
Then where we here may live long time in helth,
With moderate diet and sobrietie,
All voyd of sicknesse that farre surmounteth welth,
We rather choose to live in miserie,
And for to lacke both quietnesse and helth,
Esteeming more a gracelesse pleasure vaine,
Than for to keepe our bodies out of paine.

(94)
And where as nature doth well hir selfe content
With slender diet, wherein she most delights,
Of which hath God sufficient alwayes sent,
To serve our neede, and to refresh our sprites,
We never ceasing to feede with belly bent,
Still cramming in like greedy ravening Kites,
Both God displease, and nature quite destroy,
And for our labour lose eternall joy.

(95)
Therefore eschew thy beastly greedy minde,
This gurmandise, this filthie foule delight,

For brutish beasts, and not for men assignde,
Helpe not the flesh to overthrow the sprite,
But helpe the sprite to daunt affections blinde,
So shalt thou make both soule and body light,
When both in one shall happily agree,
To seeke the skies where thou shalt blessed bee.

(96)
Eate not to much, but often use to fast,
Both Nature biddes, and Christ commaundeth so,
Our fathers olde that lived in ages past,
Found great reliefe by this in present wo,
Who striving long thus tamed their flesh at last,
And overthrew by this their deadly fo,
Whyle as forbearing meate and sinne withall,
With fervent prayer on God they used to call.

[C5] (97)
A vertue great is abstinence no dout,
Of everie man to be esteemed much,
A helping hand to them that goe about,
The sacred skies with heavenly minde to touch,
No better fence to keepe the devill out,
No greater force, no ayde nor succor such,
Phisitions count it Natures chiefest frende,
And God himselfe doth highly it commende.

(98)
Beare of therefore and come not neare the place,
That all embrued with Gluttons bloud doth lie,
Whose soules in hell in miserable case,
With piteous plaint and howling noyse doe crie,
Lamenting sore their former lacke of grace,
While here they led their life licenciously.
When as thou hast escaped this jeopardie,
Before thy face again thou shalt descrie

(99)
A gorgeous Ile, an earthly paradyse,
Wherein there wants no kinde of pleasant sight,
No glistring show, nor costly fine devyce,
That may encrease the travailers delight,
All garnisht round with things of greatest pryce,

The sight whereof revives the gasers sprite,
Doth please the eye, and doth allure the minde
Of men that thinke safe harbour there to finde.

(100)
Of compasse large, and full of beautie faire,
The sightly show doth lie before thy face,
Which seemes as Nature there had set hir chaire,
And chosen that hir happie resting place,
From whence there comes a sweete and pleasant aire,
That farre surmounts the Amber Grece in grace,
With musicke sweete and pleasant heavenly
That round about doth in the aire resound.

[C5v] (101)
The Clives are hie, and all of Chrystall shine,
Upon the top whereof in order growes,
Hie hautie trees with majestie devine,
That glistring greene farre of in shadowes showes,
There stately stands the loftie Lordlye Pine,
With Ceders placed and Firre trees set in rowes,
Thick groves of Mirtels comly to be seene,
With coverts close of pleasant Laurell greene.

(102)
Beyond these same are mountaines rising hie,
Clad round about with trees of diverse kinde,
That placed in order much delight the eie,
And thither draw the saylers wandring minde,
Who thinke they see those hilles to touch the skie,
In vewe whereof they pleasure great doe finde,
There round about in everie place below,
Faire purple Roses joynde with Jasmins grow.

(103)
In everie place may beautie there be seene,
In everie place is pleasure for the eie,
Throughout the woods and pleasant forrests greene,
Great flocks of birdes of everie sort doe flie,
Of colours straunge and seldome to be seene,
That sit and sing upon the braunches hie,
With curious note and skilfull melodie,
Agreeing all in perfite harmonie.

(104)
No lothsome sight doth any where appeare,
No thing disordred any kinde of waye,
But all things shining there with beautie cleare,
Alluring unto pleasure and to playe,
That they that once doe chaunce to travaile neare,
Have never minde to come from thence awaye,
Such pleasure streight they doe conceyve in minde,
As no where else save there they thinke to finde.

[C6] (105)
And round about in everie place they meete,
With shalls of Mermayds swimming here and there,
Whose beautie great and pleasant singing sweete,
So daunts the eyes and eares of them that heare,
That marvaile is it if they hold their feete,
From flying over to that lustie cheare,
Their beautie is such, their voyce doth so delight,
That with their tongues they conquer everie wight.

(106)
Such is the force of this their melodie,
That long time since and many yeares ago,
The wise Ulysses when he passed bie,
Being tossed on seas and beaten to and fro,
Desirous for to heare this harmonie,
And to escape the daunger and the wo,
Stopped up his servants eares with waxe, and fast
Caused them to binde himselfe unto the Mast.

(107)
Thus sayling forward neere this pleasant place,
With wished windes and all thing serving meete,
These Mermaydes faire appeared before his face,
With shining countnance and voyces passing sweete,
There sundrie songs they song with comly grace,
And with their dities divers did him greete,
Their sweete accord and passing princely sound,
Did from the waves unto the skies rebound.

(108)
Which sound when as Ulysses streight did heare,
Could not restraine the affections of his minde,

But lowde he calles with griefe and troubled cheare,
And willes his men with haste him to unbinde,
Thus calling out and crying never the neare,
He wrests and wries all meanes he may to finde
To unlose himselfe, and striving all in vayne,
He beates his head against the Mast amayne.

[C6v] (109)
His wisdome great, could not his fancie guide,
Ne rule his minde, nor bridle his delight,
But if at libertie he had bene then untied,
He would have lept amid that pleasant sight,
And felt the fruites of pleasure at that tide,
Though it had cost him the losing of his sprite,
But being fast bound he could not have his minde,
Till sayling past it was to farre behinde.

(110)
From top of one of these same mountaines hie,
That in this Iland loftily do looke,
A river gusheth downe continuallie,
That through the valleys here and there doe crooke,
Which seemeth pleasant to the saylers eie,
That often covets to enter up the brooke,
Supposing there to finde their full delight,
Of all this gaye and gorgeous glistring sight.

(111)
Which river while they passe, on everie side,
Walke Damsels faire with beautie passing brave,
Amid the Medes with sundrie colours dide,
Of flowers fresh that fragrant odors have,
Wherof fine garlands about their heads are tide,
These oftentimes with wanton gesture wave
The passengers, alluring them to land,
With countnance sweete and becke of pleasant hand.

(112)
Not farre from thence uppon a stately roche,
Is placed strong, a sumptuous tower hie,
That doth amase the mindes that neare approche,
With beautie great that glisters in the eie,
The stately wall doth set their hart a broche,

And makes them in their course with haste to hie,
Who hoyse and hale with all the force they have,
To run themselves upon this pleasure brave.

[C7] (113)
For as the walles doe glister all of golde,
So are the Windowes all with Chrystall glased,
Whence looking out the sea men may beholde,
Such sundrie shapes as makes them all amased.
And makes them curse the time a thousand folde,
That ever upon such beautie bright they gased,
For in the end as many as there doe light,
Tormented are in miserable plight.

(114)
First taken out from out their ships they bee,
And stripped quite from all their owne aray,
And blindfeld close, so that they can not see,
Away from thence these Damsels them convay,
Unto this pyle and tower of sovereigntie,
Which seemed late to them so sweete a play,
Upon whose gates is written thus in sight,
The resting place of fleshly fond delight.

(115)
Here are they brought before this sumptuous Queene,
Who guider is and ruler of this Ile,
Who when she hath these wretched caytifes seene,
At whom with joye she scornfully doth smile,
With cruell minde and voyde of mercie cleene,
Condemnes them all to paines and torments vile,
And sundrie sentence gives on everie one,
As seemeth best unto hir selfe alone.

(116)
Some are condemned, their eyes set open wide,
Upon the colde and stonie ground to lie,
With monstrous chaines and heavie shakles tide,
Both day and night to stare continuallie
Upon the beautie that is them denide,
And call for helpe unto their enimie,
Who pleasure takes and joyeth at the hart,
To see their cruell torment and their smart.

[C7v] (117)
Some others caried forth into the wood,
With chaines are tied and fastned to the trees,
Their harts all bare and dropping downe with blood,
Their hands held up and kneling on their knees,
Are torne with Kites and Pies and Ravens wood,
That never time from feeding there doe leese,
But griping still the poore afflicted hart,
Continually augment their paine and smart.

(118)
Another sort fast in that order tide,
With torments great and miserable paine,
Against their harts a wounde made open wide,
Wherein is thrust the creature almost slaine,
Hote burning coales that readie lie beside,
Which kindle streight about the hart amaine,
The wound closde up they flame continually,
And secret burne untill the time he die.

(119)
Some sort againe by charmes enchaunted straight,
Forgo their shapes, to beasts transformed quight,
Wherein upon that Queene they still doe waight,
Somtime like Swine, and Asses oft in sight,
Somtime like Buls or Beares that dogs doe bayte,
Somtime like Lions and Tigers fierce in fight,
Such force hath fleshly pleasure in this Ile,
To alter those whom she doth thus beguile.

(120)
Yet notwithstanding continually they strive
The saylers by, who first may come a land,
With all their sayles clapped on apace they drive,
And have no feare of any shore or sand,
But while they travaile on these seas alive,
From foule delight they never turne their hand,
But forward sayle with greedie lusting minde,
Till torments due to their deserts they finde.

[C8] (121)
Alasse how great and worthie a companie,
Have here bene lost and clearely cast away,

Whose wits devine of worthie memorie,
Are talked of yet untill this present daye,
Who had escaped ech other miserie,
If on this same they had not run astraye,
Their vertues rare had alwayes glistred bright,
If that they could have shunned this foule delight.

(122)
The mightie Hercules that lived long ago,
Whose worthy actes deserve immortall fame,
Who spent his dayes in anguish and in wo,
Not bent to pleasure, nor given unto game,
But following vertue for which he travaylde so,
That still he shunned eche thing that longde to shame,
Could not escape this dreadfull daungerous place,
But lost himselfe thereon in piteous case.

(123)
The subtill wit and judgement aye profound,
That painted vertue lively to the eie,
Who shewed the harmes and hurts of vice unsound,
And opned plaine the place whereas they lie,
The selfe same man that once such favor found,
Of Delphos that he gat the soveraintie,
For wit and vertue passing everie man,
Upon this Ile yet wretchedly he ran.

(124)
A thousand such in stories olde we finde,
Of sundry like our sacred volumes tell,
That ran amisse upon this fancie blinde,
For lacke of good advise and guiding well,
Yea though they wholy did applie their minde
To everie vertue, yet on this vice they fell,
Example he with Uries wife that lay,
And eke his sonne that further ran astray.

[C8v] (125)
Amongst the daungers of these harmfull seas,
No daunger like to this there comes in sight,
That more doth worke the passengers disease,
Or drives them more to shewe their force and might,
Nor no men more the almighty Lord displease,

Than these that happen on this place to light,
Wherefore we ought with heede and carefull eie,
Farre off from hence with might and maine to flie.

(126)
And often wey the myschiefe that will ryse,
If that we leave our happy course to keepe,
For vaine delight that here deludes the eyes,
And bringeth men in restlesse rest a sleepe,
Nay rather let us these flattring showes despyse,
And seeke to scape this gulfe of daunger deepe,
Which for a litle trifling pleasure vaine,
Doth bring us unto everlasting paine.

(127)
Direct thy ship and course another way,
And still remember how happie they shall bee,
That have not falne upon this Ile astray,
Where fleshly joyes and foolish fancies bee,
But doe themselves with all their might assay,
To finde the port of true felicitie,
Eschewing everie storme and troublesome winde,
That blowes contrarie to their vertuous minde.

(128)
And wey the paines and torments they shall have,
That give themselves to follow foule delight,
And breake the lawes that God to all men gave,
How they shall wayle and howle in piteous plight,
When that their carcasse comth once to grave,
Their sinfull bodie severed from their sprite,
Which sprite shall never feele release of paine,
As long as God doth in the heavens raigne.

[D1] (129)
Though that the motions of the flesh be much,
And though that nature herein beare some sway,
Yet ought the force of reason to be such
In man, as well may put such toyes away,
The minde devine must never so basely touch,
Such things unpure as may be hir decay,
But mount aloft with wings unto the skies,
Where perfite joy and perfite pleasure lies.

(130)
For earthly joyes and fancies are unmeete,
For such as God appointes with him to live,
Who ought to abandon all such pleasures sweete,
As use wherof may them offend or grieve,
And take good heede whereas they set their fete,
Not everie show, nor everie path beleeve,
But only walke in that appointed way,
That God himselfe before their eies doth lay.

(131)
And flie the pathes, though that they pleasant seeme,
That he hath here forbidden to be trode,
And cast away all fonde affections cleene,
The weight whereof the soule so sore doth lode,
That languishing upon the earth with teene,
Constrained is it there to make abode,
And never can aspire unto the skie,
For heavie weight that doth upon it lie.

(132)
And as Ulysses passing by this place,
Where Mermayds flocke whereof we spake before,
Whose sugred songs with sweete and lovely face,
Did seeke to traine him to that deadly shore,
Did give himselfe with wise and heavenly grace,
For to withstand this lewd and flattring lore,
Compellde his men to binde him to the Mast,
Whereby with speede this daunger great he past.

[D1v] (133)
So in these seas of pleasures least we quaile,
We ought to binde our wills to reason strong,
As to the Mast that beares our chiefest saile,
That guides us best thorowout this journey long,
So shall not all these flattring showes prevaile,
So shall we scape this poysned deadly song,
That hath bewitched so many vertuous eares,
And brought them unto torments and to teares.

(134)
But if there doe such punishment remaine
For those which while they vertuous seeke to bee,

Doe fall into this lake of pleasures vaine,
Whereby they come to greatest miserie,
Condemned unto everlasting paine,
Where gastly shapes and hellish sightes they see,
Shut out for ever from that beautie bright,
That farre surmounts eche other kinde of sight.

(135)
If those I say, such torments have to taste,
What plagues are due unto that sinfull sort,
That both with minde and beastly tongue unchaste,
Of lothsome vice doe make a play and sport,
And where they ought not spende a word in waste,
Their shamelesse mouths wheresoever they doe resort,
Doth utter out the filthiest words they can,
Without respect of eyther God or man.

(136)
Contenting not themselves with wretched deedes,
Alone to passe away their sinfull race,
But with such wordes as filthily proceedes,
From out their hearts defiling everie place,
With lothsome showe as stinking noysome weedes,
That freshest flower in gardens doth deface,
So doe these beasts with tongue and talke uncleene,
Defile eche thing that fairest may be seene.

[D2] (137)
With beastly wordes that all of baudrie sound,
These Rascals vile themselves doe most delight,
Corrupting mindes that otherwise were sound,
With speach unpure, and wanton gesture light,
Wherein they are skillde as in their arte profound,
Whose tongues doe teach their vile unsaverie sprite,
Their shamelesse tongues while as their acts they tell,
Doth cause to blush the devill himselfe in hell.

(138)
Most wretched creatures that lead your lives with shame,
And die like beasts in miserable plight,
The paynes of hell is ende of all your game,
Eche damned soule shall feele his torment light,
While as they lie in never ceasing flame,

Respecting yours who for your foule delight,
Farre passe them all in torments and in paine,
This is your end and your assured gaine.

(139)
Let this suffice to give thee warning here,
That saylest neere this lewde and daungerous place,
Though that the beautie faire at first appere,
Thou seest the ende how that in wretched case,
They plagued are and buie their pleasure deare,
Regarde thy selfe and seeke for better grace,
And stay not gasing, nor venter thou to neare,
It is not good with daungers for to play,
Leave off betimes and sayle another way.

(140)
And take good heede, for straight before thy face,
Amid these seas another daunger lies,
That bearing up his head a little space,
Above the water, oft deceives the eyes,
Upon the which have died in wretched case,
A number great of men accounted wise,
The show is small that doth appeare a hie,
The chiefest daunger doth under water lie.

[D2v] (141)
The top whereof is smoothly polished,
And doth not threaten hasard with the show,
By which have many Mariners bene led,
To travaile neare the state thereof to know,
Who with their ships yllfavoredly have sped,
While as their Keeles have toucht the rocke below.
And all to torne a pieces forced to flie,
Their maisters sprawling on the surges hie.

(142)
The lustiest Mariners have bene drowned heare,
Whose Barkes have borne the bravest port on seas,
For lusty show and stomacks voyd of feare,
While as they sayled which way them best did please,
Who counsayle none, nor no advise would heare,
For warning good did ever them displease,

Still trusting to their owne deceyved wit,
From whose advise they would not stirre a whit.

(143)
Ne cast they here themselves away alone,
But cause great number more their course to misse,
Perswading them that neare unto this stone,
Doth lie the way to everlasting blisse,
Assuring them that daunger there is none,
And that themselves are well assured of this,
By which vaine words they cause the simple men,
To cast away themselves by following them.

(144)
This daungerous place that hath so many lost
And thus beguiled, is called Heresie,
A hurtfull place, a most pernicious cost,
A wofull rocke, a wretched jeoperdie,
Which oft hath hurt and quite consumed almost
The Navie faire of Christianitie,
Which gorgeous fleete had long time since bene drent,
If mightie Jove had not them succour sent.

[D3] (145)
Who pitying them of his accustomed grace,
When as they were with stormes and tempests tost,
And even at point to fall upon this place,
Where as they had bene altogither lost,
Lamenting as it were their wretched case,
To see them die that him so dearely cost,
Rebuked the winds, and tooke the helme in hand,
And brought them safe unto the assured land.

(146)
A happie guide in these so dreadfull seas,
Whose blessed aide if all men earst had sought,
With humble minde in seeking him to please,
And setting all their owne devise at nought,
They had not purchased thus their owne disease,
Nor wretchedly themselves to mischiefe brought,
Ne had they left behind them such a fame,
As hitherto the world resound with shame.

(147)
Cherinthus had not cast himselfe awaye,
Upon this rocke in miserable plight,
Nor Eutyches had passed this wretched way,
If serving God had bene his chiefe delight,
Novatus had not sayled here astray,
Nectorius had not on this mischiefe light,
Nor Arrius with his Arrians here had dide,
Nor all the swarme of Manicheys beside.

(148)
With thousands more that here I loth to name,
Who might have scaped this dredfull place full well,
That brought them unto everlasting shame,
And threw them headlong to the pit of hell,
Whereas they waile in never ceassing flame,
And for their sinnes continually doe yell,
If that they had sought this safe assured aide,
And unto him for helpe had alwayes praide.

[D3v] (149)
Take thou good heede that travailest hereby,
Least that thou fallest upon this hurtfull place,
Beware of schisme, beware of heresie,
And pray to God continually for grace,
That he may keepe thee from this miserie,
And bring thee safe unto the resting place,
In giving thee a quicke and watchfull eie,
Whereby thou mayst such covert daungers flie.

(150)
Looke well about and trust not everie sprite,
That seemes to teach the safe assured waye,
Be well assured he teach the way aright,
Or walke not thou else after him astraye,
The devill himselfe can seeme an angell bright,
The simple soule the easlier to betraye,
But Christ hath left you here his scriptures plaine,
A touchstone true to trie religion vaine.

(151)
By these examine everie prating sprite,
By these go trie what unto thee is tought,

Let these be judge who teacheth wrong or right,
Let these discerne the good things from the nought,
Of these in darkenesse borrow all the light,
Of these still let thy wavering minde be tought,
So shalt thou well be able thy selfe to trie,
Where shadowes false, and where deceit doth lie.

(152)
Beleve not those same slaundrous mouthes untrue,
Who make report how that the bookes devine,
Corrupted are with false translations newe,
Of only malice these envious beasts repyne,
They see the spirite of God will them subdue,
That in these sacred letters bright doth shine,
And therefore for to bring them in contempt,
These slaundrous lyes maliciously they invent.

[D4] (153)
As he that late such needlesse paines did take,
In culling out the faults he could espie,
Of everie tittell straight accompt doth make,
In noting where he thinkes they run awrie,
And as he thought profoundly thereof spake,
But if thou shalt his worthy judgement trie,
Thou well shalt see his fonde and foolish braine
Hath taken all his travaile here in vaine.

(154)
Beside, another marke there is to know
These wretched sprites that leades men thus to hell,
Though clad in pelts of sheepe they simple show,
And many tales of God and heaven tell,
Yet malice doth their mindes so overflow,
That all things can they not dissemble well,
Their bloudie teeth doth still appeare in sight,
Wherewith like Wolves continually they fight.

(155)
Example one amongst a number more
Let Arrius be, who whilst he here did raigne,
Of torments great and tortures had in store,
Wherewith he put true Christians still to paine,
With sundrie deaths not heard off oft before,

And griefes that newly sprang from cruell braine,
As splintars sharpe of reedes which sore did pricke,
That in their fingers twixt nayle and flesh did sticke.

(156)
That divelish minde that reigneth now in hell,
Doth still envy the happie state of man,
And since the time that first to earth he fell,
Doth labour still by all the meanes he can,
To cause them all in paines with him to dwell,
Whose cursed children as their sire began,
Continue still with rancour and with heate,
To persecute that happie heavenly seate,

[D4v] (157)
Chrysostome he that long agoe hath tride
These brittell seas and searched everie place,
Who had good proofe of everie winde and tide,
And well could sayle to finde the port of grace,
Declared which way these people might be spide,
That thus deceyve in miserable case,
And gave plaine token how we well should know
These Barks of schisme that on these seas doe row.

(158)
Did ever yet, sayth he, the simple sheepe
With bloudy mouth the greedie wolfe pursue?
Not once: But ravening wolves doe never sleepe
From hunting them. So Cain poore Abell slew,
Not Abell him, so Ismaell Isaac true
Did persecute, not Isaac him. The Jewe
Thus troubled Christ, and heretikes alway
True Christians killde, their fruits doth them bewray.

(159)
Thus plainly doth this skilfull father olde
Conclude, that such as beare such hatefull minde,
Against the flocke, and happie harmlesse folde
Of Christ, still following them with malice blinde,
To be the Wolves, of whom our Saviour tolde,
And heretikes of most pernitious kinde,
The Wolfe by ravening evermore is tride,
The Heretike by cruell minde is spide.

(160)
Then since thou mayst full well discerne this yll,
Sayle farre from thence and steare advisedly,
And guide thy selfe by good and carefull skill,
So shalt thou misse this fearefull jeoperdie,
Give not the reines nor bridle unto will,
But make it subject to the motions hie,
So shalt thou save thy selfe from daunger great,
And sooner finde the happie resting seat.

[D5] (161)
Yet once againe thou needest to take good heede,
For hereabouts an Iland faire doth lie,
That to the saylers mischiefe great doth breede,
That flames farre off like Phebus in the skie,
Which glistring sight the gasers minde doth feede,
And doth allure them for to travaile nie,
Perswading them some worthie sight is there,
That so encompast is with shining clere.

(162)
In everie place here Pyramides do rise,
With costly stones compact of gorgeous show,
Whose stately tops doe seeme to touch the skies,
The bases square are framed faire below,
With such proportions as pleaseth best the eies,
In order placed, and standing row by row,
Adourned brave with torches flaming bright,
That seeme to spoyle the day it selfe of light.

(163)
A thousand altars garnished here doe stande,
With cloth of golde and Purple passing faire,
And fiers burning hie on everie hande,
Where Incense cast doth cause a pleasant aire,
Which smelling sweete a great way from the lande,
Doth cause a number thither to repaire,
On everie altar Images appere,
Of sundrie Gods that people worship there.

(164)
There Saturne stands with envious countnance sad,
And next to him hath Jupiter his place,

And Venus smiling faire with beautie glad,
And fuming Mars with hote and fierie face,
Apollo there with glistering beames is clad,
And Dian with hir silver shining grace,
Swift Mercurie amongst them here doth stande,
With flickring wings and golden rod in hande.

[D5^v] (165)
Great Bacchus here is placed with majestie,
And neare to him Dame Ceres may be seene,
And Proserpine that low beneath doth lie,
And Juno once of heaven counted Queene,
And Berecynthya mother of the skie,
With Flora clad in lustie youthfull greene,
Here Castor joynd with Pollux faire doth stand,
And Esculapius with his snakes in hand.

(166)
On other aultars joyning thereto neare,
A number great of pictures placed bee,
That monstrous to the lookers on appeare,
As one that portred is with faces three,
An other killing dragons with a speare,
Another holding in his hand a tree,
And wading over rivers easilie,
With monstrous legs and shoulders shamefull hie.

(167)
But most of all that makes men there to muse,
There standes a saint in straunge disguised sort,
To take it for a man or woman you may chuse,
For of them both it seemes to beare a port,
Arayed in gownes as women most do use,
A Lettice cap it weares and bearde not short,
And thus disguised in straunge and masking Cotes,
Esteemes no other offring here than Otes.

(168)
A number great of such straunge pictures vaine,
Here mayst thou see, of whom I list not tell,
That unto Priests have alwayes bene a gaine,
And led such as them worshipped unto hell,
The Meschyts here of Mahomet remaine,

And all his saints to whom the Turke doth yell,
As Vanus and Sedichasis, that victorie doth bring,
With Mireschinus and Ascichum & Chidirell the king.

[D6] (169)
Before ech Image stand Tapers burning bright,
And odors sweete doe fume continually,
The people kneeling round about in sight,
With hands helde up and voyces lowde doe crie,
Eche one complayning of his wretched plight,
And seking there redresse of myserie.
Doe call upon their goddes with fervent minde,
Supposing thus a perfite helpe to finde.

(170)
This daungerous place is called Idolatrie,
Whereon are lost the Turkes and Paganes all,
That hither fast in monstrous flocks doe flie,
Not fearing mischiefe that may them befall,
And numbers great of Christians here doe die,
That leaving Christ on Idols fast doe call,
With great despite unto the almightie king,
That this detests above all other thing.

(171)
For nothing doth so much the minde offende,
Of that most sacred majestie devine,
Nor nothing makes him more his plagues to send,
Than when he sees his servants to decline
From serving him to seeke another frende,
And setting up an Idoll in his shrine,
This more doth him displease assuredly,
Than any whoredome, theft or robbery.

(172)
Him liketh to be worshipped alone,
With earnest minde and with unfeyned hart,
Who worships him must worship others none,
It is not meete for any to give part,
Of honor due to him, unto a stone,
For who so doth is like in the ende to smart,
In feeling paines and torments to them due,
That worship false and fained Gods untrue.

[D6v] (173)
This only cause did make him oft forsake
His chosen flocke the auncient Israelites,
Who though with mouth he often to them spake,
Appointing to them sacred lawes and rites,
Yet evermore his ordinances they brake,
And worshipped sundrie false and lying sprites,
In everie grove, on everie woode and hill,
They Idols placed contrarie to his will.

(174)
For which he often gave them over quite,
Into the hands of cruell enimies,
Who delt with them in miserable plight,
Still vexing them with terror and with tyrannies,
Of ech man used with foule and great despite,
Compelde to suffer thousand kinds of cruelties,
Accounted slaves and abjects clearely lost,
That earst of all men were esteemed most.

(175)
For this poore Christians often times have felt,
The usage vile, and force of Turkish hands,
That many yeares have fowly with them delt,
Depriving them of children, wife and lands,
Since first the service of Idols out they smelt,
Which brought them to captivitie and bands,
Decayed their vertues, and lost their auncient fame,
And made them to the world an open shame.

(176)
Therefore beware, and shun this filthie place,
Let Paule thy Pilot be upon these seas,
Who sayth Idolators shall never see the face
Of God, nor finde the joyfull port of ease,
For Idoll servers are quite deprived of grace,
And by no meanes the almightie Lord can please,
Such kinde of servants only he desires,
As seeke to serve him as himselfe requires.

[D7] (177)
All other service he esteemeth as vaine,
And most he hates such fond religion blinde,

As is devised by dreame of foolish braine,
That worship only doth delight his minde,
That he himselfe hath taught in scriptures plaine,
To this his servants doth he straightly binde,
Ne suffers them to honor this or that,
But plainly hath himselfe appointed what.

(178)
Serve thou him therefore as he liketh best,
With all thy hart, with all thy minde him love,
Let him be hiest alwayes in thy brest,
Take heede that none be placed him above,
Esteeme no creature so above the rest,
That love thereof shall him from thee remove,
For that beside is foule Idolatrie,
To love a worldly thing excessivelie.

(179)
Not only Imageservers have the name,
Of blinde Idolatours, but everie such,
That inwardly with fervent love doth flame,
Esteeming fading fancies here to much,
Preferring them before all feare or shame,
As those whose minds the love of God doth teach,
Or beautie faire of some excelling dame,
These kinde of loves when in the hart they lie,
Are foulest kindes of vile Idolatrie.

(180)
Farre of from this see therfore that thou flie,
If that thou meanst the haven faire to finde,
For who so toucheth on this same shall die,
In suffring shipwracke through his follie blinde,
Refuse this course, and sayle forth happily,
Keepe well the joyfull haven still in minde,
Whose pleasures great shall fully thee reward,
For all thy paines and all thy travailes hard.

[D7v] (181)
Another daunger lies there in thy way,
That seemeth good and safe unto the eie,
Whereat a number great of ships doe stay,
That here are lost or put in jeopardie,

With colour false of good it doth betray,
And cloked faire doth cause men travaile bie,
And most allures such men as seeke for fame,
Hypocrisie this mischiefe hath to name.

(182)
A rocke but soft and simple to the eie,
That pleaseth much the minde of worldlye sight,
Whereas disceyte doth closely covered lie.
Which hindreth men from travailing aright,
The place is large and riseth some thing hie,
Upon the top whereof in open sight,
There stands an Image covered all of stone,
That there was placed many yeares agone.

(183)
Which Image here I would describe to thee,
But that long since it hath bene painted plaine
By learned Chaucer that gem of Poetrie,
Who passed the reach of any English braine,
A follie therefore were it here for me,
To touch that he with pencell once did staine,
Take here therefore what he therof doth say,
Writ in the Romance of his Roses gaye.

¶ Another thing was done their write,
That seemed like an Hypocrite,
And it was cleped Pope holye,
That ill is she that privilye,
Ne spareth never a wicked deede,
When men of hir taken none heede,
And maketh hir outward precious,
With pale visage and pituous.
And seemeth a simple creature,
[D8] But there nis no misadventure,
That she ne thinketh in hir courage,
Full like to hir was thilke Image,
That maked was by hir semblance,
She was full simple of countnance,
And she was clothed and eke shod,
As she were for the love of God,
Youlden to religion,
Such seemed hir devotion,

A Psalter helde she fast in hande,
And busily she gan to fonde,
To make many a faint prayer
To God and to his saints deare,
Ne she was gaye, fresh nor jolliffe,
But seemd to be full intentiffe
To good workes and to faire,
And thereto she had on a haire,
Ne certes she was fat nothing,
But seemed werie for fasting,
Of colour pale and dead was shee,
From hir the gates aye warned bee,
Of Paradyse the blissfull place,
For such folke maken leane their grace,
As Christ sayth in his Evangile,
To get their price in towne a while,
And for a little glorie vaine,
They lesen God and eke his raigne.

(184)
Thus hath the golden pen of Chaucer olde,
The Image plaine descrived to the eie,
Who passing by long since did it beholde,
And tooke a note therof advisedly,
Unto his fellowes of that age it tolde,
And left it eke for his posteritie,
That ech man passing by might plainly know,
The perfite substance of that flattring show.

[D8v] (185)
An enmie great unto the Christian fleete,
Is this foule rocke of false Hypocrisie,
That us depriveth of the pleasure sweete.
And brings our soules to greatest miserie,
A lothsome vice, a wretched crime unmeete
For men professing Christianitie,
Eschew it then and farre off from it flie.
Let not such blinde affections bleare thy eie.

(186)
Seeke rather good to be, than good to seeme,
Seeke so to live as thou doest here professe,
So shall both God and man thee best esteeme,

So shalt thou perfite Christian life expresse,
What good doth it when men thee godly deeme,
And thou thy selfe art full of wickednesse,
Although thou mayst dissemble for a while,
Yet canst thou not no long time God beguile.

(187)
His eie doth still discerne thy inward thought,
Thy secret dealings well he doth beholde,
And all thy deedes in huckermucker wrought,
At length before the world he shall unfolde,
To what a miserie shalt thou then be brought,
When all thy faults shall openly be tolde,
When all thy filthie vices there shall smoke,
That here were hidden under godly cloke?

(188)
Christ hath us taught for to abhorre this crime,
When as he cursed the Scribes and Pharisies,
Who seemde the godliest livers at that time,
All garnished outward with Hypocrisies,
As though they daily staffe by staffe did clime,
By godly life unto the hautie skies,
Whereas their harts were full of hellish sprites,
And they themselves most cursed Hypocrites.

[E1] (189)
O what a number at this present day,
Doe swarme in everie towne, in everie place,
That God be thanked, and God be praised can say,
With gesture mylde and feyned godly grace,
Who crouching low before men fast can pray,
As if that God himselfe should stand in place,
And yet for all this show for all this goodly geare,
Disceitfull knaves at length they doe appeare.

(190)
Beguiling men that put in them their trust,
Oppressing poore men by straunge and sundrie wayes
Without all conscience, in word nor deede found just,
Yet would they seeme as though they God did prayse,
In serving him according to his lust,
Where as in deede these cursed Castawayes,

Doe never worship any God in minde,
But alwayes serve their owne affections blinde.

(191)
O sinfull beasts what meane you thus to deale,
Thus covertly before the face of God,
Be well assured you can not long conceale,
Be well assured you can not scape his rod,
Your wretched deedes in time he shall reveale,
Your sinfull life shall once be blasde abrode,
Your masking garments that you so long have worne,
Shall all be rent, and from your shoulders torne.

(192)
Your painted visard shall be plucked away,
Wherewith so many here you did deceave,
And all your curious counterfet aray,
You shalbe forced against your will to leave.
The Purple garments wherein you long did playe,
By which your honour here you did receave,
Shall off be plucked, and all things else beside,
And then the bare arsed Ape shall plaine be spide.

[E1v] (193)
Sayle thou not neare this wretched cursed place,
That seekest the happie haven for to finde,
Crie out to God and call for better grace,
Commit thy sayles unto a better winde,
Eschew the looke of false dissembling face,
Use vertue alwayes with unfained minde,
So shalt thou sooner finde the port of blisse,
That cursed Hypocrites assuredly shall misse.

(194)
Now veer thy sheates, hale up thy Mainsayle hie,
Advaunce thy tops, hang out thy flags abroade,
The greatest daunger hast thou travailde by,
And neare thou art unto the happie roade,
The other perils that in the way doe lie,
May well be passed, and well be overtrode,
For none do perish heare in any place,
But such as are both voide of wit and grace.

(195)
Cast feare away, and take a lustie hart,
Revive thy spirites with gladnesse and with joy,
Cheare up thy minde, and comfort everie part,
Remove ech griefe that may thy sense anoy,
For neare unto the haven now thou art,
Where pleasure dwelles and everlasting joy,
Whereas thou shalt the almightie father see,
The spring and head of all felicitie.

(196)
Although these daungers that hereabout doe lie,
Doe never hurt the godly carefull minde,
Yet for their safeties that here shall travaile bie,
I briefly will declare their names and kinde,
That sooner so they may such mischiefes flie,
Not running rashly on these mischiefes blinde,
But keeping still the safe assured seas,
They sooner may finde out the port of ease,

[E2] (197)
The first and worst of these same daungers great,
Is blasphemie, a foule and filthie crime,
Which barketh still against the heavenly seat,
And most offends the majestie devine,
With fearefull othes sworne out in furie great,
Of Reprobates the most assured signe,
The damned sprites continually doe sweare,
Without respect of any godly feare.

(198)
Next this hath carlish crueltie the place,
A mischiefe that doth hellish mindes assayle,
With lothsome looke and foule and deadly face,
Whereon a number great of ships doe quayle,
That wanting gentle windes and voyde of grace,
To neare this dreadfull daunger hastily sayle,
Whereas they leese themselves in wretched plight,
And never finde the blisfull haven bright.

(199)
Then hatred showes his hurtfull head aloft,
A hatefull harme, and hurtfull unto many,

Which overthroweth the suttle sayler oft,
And drowneth deepe the spitefull companie,
Who while they deeme the bed of malice soft,
Doe rest themselves upon this miserie,
Brought here a sleepe with fonde malitious minde,
They never seeke the haven faire to finde.

(200)
Here Murder all embrued with bloud doth stand,
That gives unto the eye a fearefull sight,
On top whereof with shaking sword in hand,
Is Furie placed, a foule deformed sprite,
Who suffers none to attaine the happie land,
That once upon this mischiefe happes to light,
The Fiend himselfe that guides the damned raigne,
First found this place and hither brings his traine.

[E2v] (201)
Hereby stands theft a foule and foolish yll,
That doth allure the greedie gracelesse minde,
Traynde up from youth in witlesse wretched will,
And robberie, sister to this vice by kinde,
May here be seene about hir swarming still,
These lustie blouds that here will soner finde
A pound, than lose a penie willinglye,
Who riding here at oken ancour lye.

(202)
Not farre from thence stands sinfull sorcerie,
A mischiefe founded by the devill first,
With charmes enchantments and astrologie,
The practisers whereof are all accurst,
And joynd with this, stands infidelitie
Togither linked as of all other worst,
The one thinkes all things by the starres are donne,
The other that all at randon here doth ronne.

(203)
To this apace our learned maisters hie,
That teach us what shall happen yeare by yeare,
And what sore plagues are threatned from the skie,
As famine, warres and other pituous geare,
Great learned Clarks and such as seldome lie,

As by their worthy doings doth appeare,
Who faine would be esteemed cunning men,
While as they steale the fruits of others pen.

(204)
Now last of all two daungers great appeare,
Betweene the which thou canst not choose but run,
Therefore thou must looke circumspectly here,
As other saylers heretofore have done,
Sayle just betweene them both, sayle not to neare
To any of them, for strong the tide doth run,
And often drives the heedlesse Barkes thereon,
That in the middle safely might have gon.

[E3] (205)
The one of them with lofty looke doth rise,
And seemes to touch the place where saints doe dwell,
All blacke the other lies before the eies,
The plateforme plaine and Image right of hell,
There shalt thou heare continuall shrikes and cries
Of damned soules that piteously doe yell,
And lothsome showes and shapes doth eke appeare,
Of cursed sprites that hover here and there.

(206)
Presumption hath the one of these to name,
That makes men like their doings here to well,
The other Desperation full of blame,
That throwes men headlong to the pit of hell,
Two mischiefes great that mans destruction frame,
And makes men low with damned sprites to dwell,
These are the hurts that in these seas doe lie,
Regarde them well and warely from them flie.

(207)
Remaineth nothing for thee nowe behinde,
But gracious markes that leade the sayler right,
That comforts much the godly vertuous minde,
And teacheth them to finde the port of light,
Passe thou by these, so shalt thou surely finde,
The chiefest succour for the werie sprite,
For who so runnes by these shall never misse,
The haven faire of everlasting blisse.

(208)
The formost of these sure and happie guides,
Is earnest Prayer that gives a goodly show,
And keepeth safe the Barke from troublous tides,
That moved with hellish tides contrarie flow,
In safetie here the wandring vessell rides,
Whatsoever hap, what winde soever blow,
Though devill, world, and flesh against it strive,
Yet under sayle it safely here may drive.

[E3v] (209)
A thousand happy hands may here be seene,
Helde up with hart unfeyned unto the skies,
Washed in the waters of repentance cleane,
And purged pure with teares of weeping eies,
A thousand tongues from mindes that well doe meane,
Yeelde up to God their fervent suites and cries,
At morning, noone and night continuallye,
Here shalt thou see them on their faces lye.

(210)
The next is Peace, a quiet happie place,
Where as no strife nor rancor can be found,
Rest thou thy Barke within this roade of grace,
And travaile for to touch upon this ground,
They alwayes come to good that run this race,
Thou needest not here for feare of daunger sound,
For those that here most peaceably remayne,
Have daily traffique with the heavenly raigne.

(211)
Hereby doth Love another beautie stand,
That brings thee streight unto the rode of rest,
And poynteth out directly with hir hand,
The perfite way by which thou mayst be blest,
No harmfull Boate may ever here take land,
But only those that please the almightie best,
And seeke to sayle according to his will,
This Love doth all the hestes of God fulfill.

(212)
Next Mercie stands, a goodly marke and plaine,
That leadeth streight unto the blissfull port,

And is possessed of the heavenly traine,
And most frequented of the vertuous sort,
Who doe not thinke the words were spoken in vaine,
Wherewith our Saviour did the Jewes exhort,
Assuring those that mercie shewde to men,
That mercie should be shewed againe to them.

[E4] (213)
Not farre from hence may Pacience plaine be seene,
The Bulwarke strong against all injurie,
The sovereigne Ladie and most victorious Queene,
In trouble, toyles and worldly miserie,
Which evermore assuredly hath beene
The Buttresse chiefe of Christianitie,
By which the soules of vertuous men have saylde,
That never yet in storme or tempest quaylde.

(214)
Here lively Faith may well discerned bee,
The chanell safe that leades to heavenly blisse,
Whereby the Fathers olde attainde to see,
The haven faire and port of perfite blisse,
This made the Martyrs flame in such degree,
That life they weyed not in respect of this,
By which they knew assuredly to finde,
The blissfull place conceyved in their minde.

(215)
These are the markes whereto thou must take heede,
By these thou mayest thy selfe in voyage guide,
If that thou seekest luckily to speede,
To passe the flattes and scape the raging tide,
Upon this course have Mariners agreed,
That long time since these seas have fully tride,
No other way they here have left behinde,
Whereby we may the happie haven finde.

(216)
Sayle therfore as the perfite course doth lie,
And run the race that is to thee assignde,
For who so runneth otherwise awrie,
The haven faire of blisse shall never finde,
But drownde in seas for evermore shall die,

With torments great and death of dreadfull kinde,
Where they that kepe the course that Christ hath tought
Shall unto everlasting joyes be brought.

[E4v] (217)
Here would I playne set out before thine eies,
This happie place, wherein thy Barke shall rest,
What show it hath, and in what sort it lies,
But that it can by no man be exprest,
That place of joy above the starrie skies,
Appointed only for the godly and blest,
By any wit can not be throwly scand,
Ne can be blasde by any mortall hand.

(218)
The joyes are such as cannot here be tolde,
No pen can paint, nor tongue can tell the kinde,
The gorgeous sight that saints shall here beholde,
Surmounts the reach of any earthly minde,
And passeth aye a hundreth thousand folde,
The sweetest pleasures that in thys world we finde,
No eye hath seene, no eare hath ever harde,
The joyes that are for godly men preparde.

(219)
Applie thy minde to seeke this happy place,
Put all thy strength and all thy force thereto,
Call unto God continually for grace,
As Christ hath taught, seeke alwayes for to doe,
Set alwayes him and his before thy face,
So shalt thou come the blessed haven to,
So thou thy selfe with eyes shalt plainly see,
What joy, what pleasures there preparde bee.

Τελος,

[E5]

The death of S.Polycarpus *Bishop of Smyrna, and* disciple to saint John. *Euseb.lib.4.*

WHen fierce Alecto moved the mindes
of gracelesse wicked men,
To persecute the sacred Church
of Christ beginning then,
And all the furies breaking loose
from hell with cancred spite,
Did seeke by all the meanes they could,
to quench that heavenly light,
The poore afflicted Christian flocke
was spoyled on everie side,
And everie wolvish tongue and tooth,
in bloud of saints was dide.
Ech vertuous man tormented was,
and godly men were slaine,
And havocke made of holy harts,
with hatred and disdaine,
The worthie father Polycarp,
a man of auncient yeares,
With aged countnance beautified,
and deckt with silver heares,
Was sought for now and followed fast
with foote of cruell foe,
No place of safegard left for him,
nor path of peace to goe,
In everie place was watch and warde,
and spials out were sent,
By bloudie suite to overthrow
and trap the innocent,

But he not moved with all this rage,
In quiet doth remaine,
[E5v] Accounting life and pleasures lost,
for Christ his chiefest gaine,
Yet following counsell of his frendes,
unto a secret place,
He doth depart, and quietly
remaining there a space,
With humble heart doth call to God,
and prayeth continually,
For christian Church, his friends and such
as live in miserie,
For thus he used evermore
throughout all his life to praye,
Continuing with his godly friends,
in prayer night and daye.
Thus three dayes hole in prayer past,
he takes at length his rest,
And whilst upon his bed he lies,
with quiet sleepe possest,
Him seemeth in his dreame hee sees
the Pillow all on flame,
That round about encompasseth
his head upon the same,
Which blasing round about the bed
with firie countnance bright,
In little time as thought him then,
consumes the Bolster quight,
Awaking from this fearefull dreame,
He lifteth up his hed,
Declareth that this vision straunge
of firie flaming bed,
Doth plainly show that shortly he
must lose his life in fire,
And leave his aged limmes in flame,
for Christ his chiefe desire,
Yet once againe at friends request,
from thence he flies away,
[E6] In seeking out some covert place,
the safer for to pray,
Yet ceaseth not the tyrants foote
for to pursue him still,

But ransacking in everie place,
the guiltlesse bloud to spill,
Findes out at length the happie house
wherin this father good,
Had entred for to scape the hands
of Sathans cursed brood,
The day was almost at an ende
and sunne declining fast,
Upon the foming Occean seas,
his eyes began to cast,
When as the cursed Catchpolles found
this sacred secret place,
They make no more, but up they hie,
with swift and hastie pace.
A Garret was there placed aloft,
where as this vertuous man,
Lay quietly upon his bed,
not fearing daunger than,
The aged father riseth up
and meetes his enimies,
With countnance comly to beholde,
in sweete and pleasant guise,
Whereat the messengers amased
doe wonder verie much,
That such a worthie father olde,
of grace and goodnes such,
Should thus be sought for in this sort
by cruell tyrannie,
And well deserving long to live,
should thus untimely die.
His youth in vertue alwayes spent,
his age in honor led,
[E6v] Deserved with better quietnesse,
to rest his horie head,
But he not weying force of man,
nor cruell enimie,
Embracing tokens true of death,
determineth to die.
Such was his love to Christ his Lorde,
that through this vale of strife,
By death he rather followes him,
than him forsakes for life.

No torment of the tyrants hand,
nor feare of cruell smart,
Could once amase his vertuous minde,
nor daunt his sacred hart,
He willes them straight to lay the borde,
and for to bring him meate,
And to his foes as to his friends,
Appointeth ghestly seate,
Desiring them but libertie
to pray an houres space,
Which once obtainde he falleth downe,
and groveling on his face,
In such a comly sort he prayes,
that all that present stood,
Amased were, and even those
that sought to shed his blood,
To take him there repented much,
that they had travailde so,
In hunting for so good a man,
of force commaunded tho,
They soried much that they should take
and bring to cruell paine
So sweete a servant of the Lordes,
so vertuous and so plaine,
His prayer fully finished then,
His time was now at hand,
[E7] Upon an Asse they hoyst him up,
and compast with their bande,
They lead him toward the citie streight,
upon the Sabboth day.
Thus in his journey travailing,
there meetes him on the way,
One Herode that Lieutenant was,
Nicetas eke with him,
That father of this Herod was,
and causing him come in,
Unto the chariot where they sat,
still passing on their way,
They him perswade to cast off Christ,
and on this sort they say,
What hurt or perill can it be,
what yll can thus arise,

In calling of the Emperour God,
and offring sacrifice.
Lo this is all that thou shalt doe,
what matter great is this?
What fault can herewithall be found,
what thing is here amisse?
By doing thus thou savest thy life,
and all thy friends shalt please,
And spend thy aged yeares in rest,
and passe thy time in ease.
These words with silence first he heard,
and as they yet proceede,
What needes more words than these, saith he,
I will not doe this deede,
Ne will I call your Emprour God,
nor offer sacrifice,
In vaine you me disswade, my minde
is settled otherwise.
Offended with this aunswere much,
they both began to frowne,
[E7v] And with despite from out the Coche
they threw him headlong downe,
The fall did hurt him verie sore,
but nothing him dismay,
For chearfully as voyde of hurt,
he holdeth on his way
Unto the place where he should die,
beset on everie hand,
With swarmes and throng of people rude,
that gasing on him stand,
Whereto as soone as he was come,
this voyce from heaven fell,
Be of good comfort Polycarpe
and keepe thy conscience well.
No kinde of thing coulde there be seene,
yet many heard the voyce
That loving him and fearing God
did much thereat rejoyce,
The beastly people rayled at him
when as he came in sight,
And blasphemed God, defacing him
with words of great despight.

Thus brought among these gredie wolves
the simple sheepe doth stand,
The Judge commaunding silence streight,
with lifting up his hand,
Demaundes if that be he that Po-
lycarpus hath to name,
Whereto he boldly aunsweres him,
I am the verie same,
Then of thy selfe have some regarde,
good father olde, sayth hee.
And have respect unto thy yeares
and to thine owne degree.
Thy reverent age deserves good lucke
cast not thy selfe away,
[E8] But worship thou the Emperour
and wish him well alway,
And crie away with all such beasts
as doe no God regarde,
Then turning to the people streight,
and willing to be harde,
Olde Polycarpe with frowning looke
and hand held up to skies,
Cries out amaine away with such
as God doe here despise,
The Ruler speaking still and saying,
love Cesar with thy hart,
And blaspheme Christ, then shalt thou at
thy pleasure hence depart.
I have, sayth Polycarpus, served
Christ fourescore yeares and more,
And unto mee in all this space,
he did no hurt. Wherfore
Should I then him blaspheme that hath
bene all thus while my frende,
Whose blessed ayde from everie harme,
did alwayes me defend,
I can not serve him in such sort,
that hath so friendly delt
With me through all my life, by whom
I have such goodnesse felt,
I am a Christian I confesse,
a Christian will I die,

Come paine or joy, come death or life,
I will it not denie,
And if thou seekest the happie state,
of Christians for to know,
Their whole beliefe, and vertuous sect,
I plainly will thee show,
Whensoever thou shalt appoint the time.
Nay sayth the Judge, declare
[E8v] Before the people present here,
in all things how they fare,
Quoth he, I have thee answerde full,
in scriptures are we tought,
To give you Rulers honor such,
as unto you we ought,
We worship Princes evermore,
as Gods Lieutenants here,
And them obey, so that they bid
not things repugnant cleare
Against the lawes of God himselfe,
but for to come taccount,
Before these raging people rude,
whose madnesse doth surmount,
Their senselesse wits, it is no part
of mine I you assure,
Nor never will I doe it whilst
my life doth here endure.
Wild beasts here have I quoth the Shrife,
whereto thou shalt be cast,
Then let them lose sayth he, my words
shall stand as they have past,
I can not chaunge from good to evyll,
more meete this sinfull brood,
Should leave their lewde and beastly life,
and chaunge from evill to good.
Well quoth the Shrife offended much
and boyling all in ire,
Though thou regardst not force of beasts,
thou shalt be burnt with fire,
Thy aged bones and werish limmes,
consumde to coales shall bee,
And life (the fruite of thy contempt)
shall passe in flame from thee.

Thou threatnest me (quoth he againe)
with feeble fire and vaine,
[F1] Which as it quickly kindleth here,
so quickly dies againe,
Not knowing of the dreadfull flames
that burne continually,
Prepared for the wicked sort,
that here in sinne doe die.
But wherefore seemest thou thus to stay?
put beasts or fire to me,
With torments I nor fearefull sights
can never moved be.
These words and other like to these
him Polycarpus tolde,
With joyfull looke. The Shrife amased,
to heare his aunsweres bolde,
A Baily to the people sent,
and willes him to proclaime
That Polycarpe had thrice confest
himselfe a Christian plaine.
Which when the multitude had heard
of Jewes and Gentiles vaine,
That present were with furie great,
thus crie they out amaine,
Lo this is he that doth seduce
all Asia round about,
The father and the chiefest guide,
of all the Christian rout,
The great defacer of our Gods,
who teacheth not to make
Nor offer sacrifice, but Gods
and goodnesse to forsake.
This sayd, they crie for fire streight,
and here and there they run,
And ech man busieth much himselfe,
to see the slaughter done,
And wood from everie place they bring,
and reedes in order laye,
[F1v] And pile up fagots fast thereon,
With all the hast they may,
And thus the stake is streight preparde,
the father brought thereto,

With willing minde and joyfull hart,
his garments doth undo,
And stripes himselfe into his shirt,
while as the standers by,
Doe drive in staples to the stake,
the safer him to tie.
These chaines, quoth he, are needlesse here
for he that me doth make
To abide the fire, shall give me grace
to stand untide at stake,
Wherewith they let the chaines alone,
and tie him slenderly,
With little Hempen cordes that were
prepared speedily.
Thus like a Ram drawne from the flocke
for sacrifice he stands,
And to the heavens casting up
his eyes and holy hands,
These words with fervent mind he spake,
O God of power devine,
That Father art of Jesus Christ,
by which deare sonne of thine,
Of thee the knowledge we attaine
thou Lord of Aungels all,
Of powers and strengths & every wight,
that unto thee doe call,
The only God of righteous men,
to thee great thanks I give
That thus thou hast permitted me,
untill this day to live,
Whereby of Christ thy only sonne,
I shall a witnesse bee
[F2] With whom I trust, and thorow him,
thy blessed face to see,
The chiefest comfort of my soule,
and longing of my sprite,
Wherein eche poore afflicted hart,
doth set his whole delight,
A pleasing sacrifice I trust,
I shalbe unto thee,
That doth respect the loving hart
and minde of eche degree,

My soule through flames to thee I yeelde
that art my only light,
Receive it Lord and graunt it rest,
before thy sacred sprite,
Even as thou hast appointed, and
determind long ago,
Ech thing thou hast performed here,
and all things ordred so,
O God thou righteous art and just,
deceite is none with thee,
Therefore I render thankes and prayse,
unto thy majestie,
Through Jesus Christ the eternall God,
thy deare and only sonne,
Whose presence here to judge the world,
I trust shall shortly come.
To whom with thee and the holy sprite,
be prayse both now and then,
And laude and glory yeelded up,
for evermore. Amen.
No sooner had he done but that
These wretches voyde of grace,
Thrust fire in on everie side,
and kindling it apace,
The flame a loft beginnes to mount,
and threates the hawtie skies,
[F2v] With crooked compasse to enclose,
the martyr standing there,
Whose bodie seemed to give the showe
of golde in fornace cleare,
From whence beside there round about
a pleasant odor past.
As if some Baume or Frankincense,
had bene in fire cast,
The sinfull sort perceyving thus,
the body to remaine
Untoucht of fire, and that their toyle
and travaile was in vaine,
Doe straight commaund the hangman with
his sword to thrust him in,
Wherwith the bloud with purple streams
apace begins to spin,

And gusheth out so fast abrode,
    that even the raging flame
In divers places of the pile
    was quenched with the same,
The people all amased, depart,
    the corse neglected lies,
The soule rejoycing at this day,
    unto the heaven flies.

A Priest of Apollo straunge-
ly converted. Euseb.lib.4.

UPon the Alpes those stately mountaines hie,
Sometime there stode a gorgeous temple faire,
Whereto the people used commonly
To heare the doome of Phebus to repaire,
[F3] Wherein there lived a Priest of passing fame,
Who used to keepe the altars trim and fine,
And well could cast the sacrifice in flame,
And order all things in their course and time,
It chaunced that here passed by this way,
One Gregorie, a christian Bishop olde,
Who entred in whereas this person lay,
And lodged there all night to scape the colde,
Good entertainment gave the Priest him tho,
And used him well according to his guise,
And tolde him all in order so and so,
How Phebus there was served and in what wise,
What numbers great did seeke him day by day,
And what great store of people round about,
Were satisfied when as they came that way,
And answerde full to everie kinde of dout,
The next day when the sunne doth give his light,
The ghest departs and biddes his Host adew,
And thanks him for his lodging that same night,
And prayse good lucke of their acquaintance new,
Unto the Church the Priest in haste doth hie,
And offers up his costly sacrifice
He downeward falles and on his face doth lie,
And prayeth to his God in humble wise,
And counsell asks of divers weightie things,
What best for to be done in this or that.
Whilst of his prayers thus the temple rings,
This golden God that on the altar sat

Ne spake a worde, nor gave him any signe,
Of prayers heard as he before had done,
His tongue was tide he could not now devine,
What happened had or what thing was to come,
With countnance sad the Priest doth home depart,
And museth at this straunge and sodeine chaunce,
Laments the case with mourning heavy hart,
And fares as one beside himselfe in traunce,
[F3v] Thus heavily he spends the day away,
And when the night with shadow darke was come,
And time for everie man to goe to rest,
While on his bed he doth begin to slome,
Lo streight appeares his God all rudely drest,
With ernfull looke and thus to him he spake,
What meanst thou thus to vexe thy troubled sprite,
For pleasing me whose force is now so weake,
That scarsly can I holde my selfe upright,
That wretched ghest whom thou this other night
So entertaynst, hath me thus foule disgraced,
Hath stayed my tong, and wrought me this despite,
By whom for ever am I cleane defaced,
Nor in my temple can I lenger set,
Nor aunswere thee as I have done before
Except of him thou licence for me get,
Thou knowest my staye, torment thy selfe no more,
The Priest awakes, and soone he leaves his bed,
And followes fast his late departed ghest,
Treades out the path which he before did tred,
And pauseth not, nor doth entend to rest,
Till he him find, whom soone he overtakes,
And humbly doth him of his helpe require,
And true report of everie thing he makes,
What dolefull chaunce hath happened in his quire,
And what mishap unto his God befell,
And how his gaines are gone from him thereby
With ruthfull looke amased doth he tell,
Beseecheth him to helpe him speedily,
And to restore to him his God againe,
Which otherwise would be his great decay,
If that he should with silence thus remaine,
He willes him to remember that same day,
Wherein he werie to his house did come,

How that ech friendship then that in him lay,
He shewed him there, and how ech thing was done.
[F4] The gentle ghest his Host doth not forget
But for to shew him frendship like againe,
Unto the paper straight his hand doth set
And thus he writes in letters faire and plaine,
Unto Apollo Gregorius greeting sendes,
I give thee leave, doe as thou didst before.
With this he makes his Hoast a full amends,
Who thanketh him with all his hart therefore,
And home he comes as fast as he may fling,
And of his Church the doore he opens wide,
And unto Phebus doth the letter bring,
Upon the Altar layes it him beside,
The Idoll streight beginnes againe to prate,
And answere gives as he was wont to doe,
And prophecies of his and his estate,
Of subtile oracles disclosing one or two,
The Priest beginnes to alter his intent,
And to himselfe he mutters in his minde,
That this straunge power is only to him lent,
And graunted by some force of hier kinde,
He deemes his Gods authoritie but small,
That thus is ruled by a mortall Wight,
Nor lenger meanes he unto him be thrall,
That is obedient to another sprite,
He takes his letter and hies him thence apace,
And biddes both Church and God adew for aye,
Comes streight to Gregorie, and telleth him the case,
And prayes him for to shew him plaine the way,
By true religion to worship God on hie,
And doth repent his former wretched trade,
And all his life spent in ydolatrie,
Wherein he list not lenger for to wade,
Thus falling flat on ground before his feete,
The other gently doth him there receave,
And showes the effect of Christs commaundment sweete,
And willes him thereto earnestly to cleave,
[F4v] Who after that he had a while profest,
The Christian law, and sweete religion taught,
Tooke such delight therein that all the rest
Of fancies vaine he left and set at naught,

Embraced Christ, and served him faithfully,
And in such sort that when this Gregorie dide,
As Pastor chiefe his roome he did supply,
And happily his happie flocke did guide.

FINIS.

Plate III

Emblem LXXXIV, *Auaritia*, from Andrea Alciato, *Emblematum liber* (Antwerp: Christopher Plantin, 1577), 306.
By kind permission of the Librarian, Glasgow University Library.

Plate IV

In repetundos, et adulatores, from Henry Peacham, *Minerva Britanna* (London: Walter Dight, 1612), 115.
By kind permission of the Librarian, Glasgow University Library.

Plate V

Emblem CXV, *Sirenes*, from Andrea Alciato, *Emblematum liber* (Antwerp: Christopher Plantin, 1577), 390.
By kind permission of the Librarian, Glasgow University Library.

Plate VI

Emblem CII, *Quae supra nos, nihil ad nos*, from Andrea Alciato, *Emblematum liber* (Antwerp: Christopher Plantin, 1577), 348.
By kind permission of the Librarian, Glasgow University Library.

TEXTUAL NOTES

Epistle dedicatory
I left them. Copytext, *I left then*.

"The Ship of safegarde"
St. 18 (l. 143): *and*. Copytext, *aud*.
St. 32 (l. 251): O. Copytext *Of*.
St. 147 (l. 1174): *Novatus*. Copytext *Nonatus*.
Interpolation (l. 1479): *That maked was by hir semblance*. In copytext, *by* is *byt*.
St. 196 (l. 1603): *mischiefes*. Copytext *mischifefes*.
St. 206 (l. 1683): *Two*. Copytext *To*.
St. 207 (l. 1687): *behinde*. Copytext *bebinde*.

"The death of S. Polycarpus"
L. 46: *countnance*. Copytext *countance*.

EXPLANATORY NOTES

With a few exceptions, archaic expressions are defined in these notes only the first time they occur. See the Glossary Index to locate the definitions. Definitions are mainly drawn from the *Oxford English Dictionary*, supplemented by other standard references and contextual implications. Full publication data on works cited in abbreviated form in these notes can be found in the ensuing list of works consulted.

To the Reader.

This poem, excluding its title, is set in italics in the original. It was customary, due to the narrow page width and comparatively wide typefaces used in the 1560s, to set poems written in fourteener couplets in lines broken after the fourth foot, yielding the measure of "eight and six" mentioned by Peter Quince the carpenter in *A Midsummer Night's Dream* (3.1.22). In the present text, the practice is followed for "To the Reader" and "The death of S. Polycarpus."

The opening metaphor of life being the choice between two paths, one broad but erroneous and one narrow but virtuous, derives from Christ's parable in Matthew 7.14, which in turn was an assimilation of a Pythagorean concept. The idea had additional currency in the ancient Tablet of Cebes traditions, the best known English expression of which is William Marshall's frontispiece to George Wither's *Collection of Emblemes* (1635). For discussions of the Tablet of Cebes trope, see Chew, *Pilgrimage of Life*, 206–9; and Bath, *Speaking Pictures*, 111–15; and more generally Schleier, *Tabula Cebetis*; and *Cebes' Tablet*.

L. 7: *stayes*. Googe often uses the singular verb form to agree with a plural subject, as was common and accepted in his day.

L. 12: *tone*. One (a common formation, now archaic, apparently derived from misunderstanding "that one" as "the tone").

"The Ship of safegarde"

Sts. 2 and 3 (ll. 9–24): Googe establishes the characteristics of the Christian sailor: he eschews idleness and is impatient for gaining the heavenly port. This sentiment owes much to the medieval notion of *contemptus mundi,* the philosophy that emphasized the transience of all earthly pleasures and advocated contemplation of the life to come.

St. 5 (l. 34): *foyst.* A light galley; a vessel propelled by sails and oars.

(l. 35): *pelfe.* Wealth, goods, trash, frippery.

St. 6 (l. 46): *thwackt.* Beaten or stricken vigorously; packed or crowded.

St. 7 (l. 54): *Them selfe.* Itself.

St. 8 (l. 61): *lets.* Hindrances.

(l. 63): *Marrocke.* Morocco, referring to the Straits of Gibraltar.

(l. 64): *race of Britaine.* The English Channel, a notoriously hazardous waterway.

(l. 64): *Charybdis, nor Scyll.* Charybdis and Scylla. According to Greek legend, Charybdis was a whirlpool off the Sicilian coast situated close to Scylla, a sea monster that preyed on passing shipping. Scylla was later transformed into a rock. In *Odyssey* 12, Odysseus has to brave a middle course between these two perils.

St. 9 (l. 70): *bet.* Past participle of *to beat;* i.e., beaten.

Sts. 11 and 12 (ll. 81–96): This invocation of the Holy Ghost to aid Googe in his poetic labors is a Christian adaptation of the classical invocation of the Muse. Similar passages occur in *The Faerie Queene, Paradise Lost,* and elsewhere in Renaissance literature.

St. 11 (l. 82): *his.* Its.

St. 12 (l. 93): *Thou onlye art the starre . . . .* An identification of the Holy Ghost with moral navigation, but perhaps also an implied denial of the Morning Star Lucifer's ability to guide man to virtue.

(l. 95): *cast down thy beames.* Googe seeks the illumination of knowledge, but may also allude here and in st. 11 to the Star of Bethlehem or even to the Pentecostal tongues of flame episode in Acts 2.1–12, where the Apostles are empowered with evangelical zeal and ardor.

St. 14 (ll. 105–12): Googe presents the first of his hazards, the Rock of Pride. The traditional primacy of this vice is appropriate: the sin of Pride, or Presumption, caused Lucifer's rebellion in heaven and Adam's weakness in Eden. That Pride should be figured as a rock is iconographically just. The Greek story of Niobe tells how her pride before the gods led to Apollo and Diana's transforming her into a rock. In Alciato's emblem *Superbia,* Pride is represented as a rock because of its "hardness of countenance and such feelings as exist in a stone" (*Latin Emblems,* 67). For a full discussion of the traditions surrounding *Superbia*, see Chew, *Pilgrimage of Life*, 95–100.

(l. 110): *eche degree*. All social ranks are susceptible to this vice.

(ll. 111–12): *The compasse . . . starrie skie*. The physical bulk of the rock is itself an aspect of Pride. It is tall because it is overreaching and self-important, but its vastness also reflects its ubiquity and universality.

St. 15 (l. 114): *pouldred*. Powdered, spangled.

St. 16 (l. 122): *reach*. Headland, promontory.

St. 18 (ll. 137–44): The biblical type of the fall of Lucifer is here made explicit.

(l. 142): *foyle*. An overthrow, a repulse.

(ll. 143–44): *The chiefe estates . . . know*. A standard warning to the ruling classes to eschew Pride (cf. Lydgate's *The Fall of Princes* and Baldwin's *Mirror for Magistrates*).

St. 19 (l. 148): *to torn*. Torn to bits. Similar uses of the *to-* prefix later in the text are not glossed.

(ll. 150–52): *Like Parrats . . . bared brest*. The parrot's fine plumage makes it a type for *gloria*. Philip Stubbes shared Googe's misgivings that physical decoration was symptomatic of moral degeneracy: "the trimming and tricking of their heds, in laying out their hair to the shewe, which of force must be curled, frisled and crisped, laid out (a World to see) on wreathes & borders from one eare to an other. And least it should fall down it is vnder propped with forks, wyers & I can not tel what, rather like grime sterne monsters, then chaste christian matrones" (*Anatomie of Abuses*, F2v). Googe's passage recalls the "Lordes and Ladies" in Spenser's House of Pride who

> . . . deuise
> Themselues to setten forth to straungers sight:
> Some frounce their curled haire in courtly guise,
> Some prancke their ruffes, and others trimly dight
> Their gay attire. (*FQ* 1.4.14)

St. 20 (ll. 153–60): The equation of a fondness for fine apparel with homosexuality was common: "But nowe through our fond toyes and nice inuentions, we haue brought our selues into suche pusillanimitie, and effeminat condition, as we may seeme rather nice dames, and yonge gyrles, than puissante agents, or manlie men, as our forefathers haue bene" (Stubbes, *Anatomie of Abuses*, E2v). The evils of titivation were regarded as not only moral, but social: Thomas Lever warns that "the more gorgeous you youre selues bee in silkes-and [sic] veluettes, the more shame is it for you to see other poore and neady, beying members of the same bodye, in ragges and clothe, yea bare and naked" (*Fruitfull sermon*, 47). Tamsyn Williams discusses the Puritan perception of finery in "Polemical Prints of the English Revolution" in Gent and Llewellyn, *Renaissance Bodies*, 89–91.

St. 21 (l. 162): *staring top.* Hair standing on end.

St. 22 (l. 169): *As painted tombes. . . .* The image is from Matthew 23.27.

(l. 169): *stinch.* Variant spelling of *stench,* foul odor.

(l. 170): *Arras faire.* Handsome tapestry (as from the Arras region in northeastern France)—a commonplace metaphor for duplicity, since tapestries can act as a fair front for moldy, dank stonework.

St. 26 (l. 202): *Strike thou thy sayles.* Lower sails, as perhaps in a sign of surrender.

St. 28 (ll. 217–24): the transitory nature of physical beauty is treated elsewhere by Googe, e.g., in "To Mistress A." (*Eclogues* 91).

St. 30 (l. 236): *Tantalus.* The story of Tantalus, who, in punishment for offending the gods, was placed in a pool of water overhung with fruit trees from which he could neither eat nor drink, was a popular motif with emblem writers. See, for example, Alciato, *Latin Emblems*, 85; Palmer, *Emblems of Thomas Palmer*, 37; and Whitney, *Choice of Emblemes*, 74. See Plate III.

St. 31 (l. 245): *fret.* Eaten away, corroded.

(l. 247): *tho.* Then.

St. 33 (l. 263): *harbrow.* Harbor, from obs. harborough.

St. 34 (ll. 265–73): The ship encounters the second hazard, the Rock of Avarice, or Greed. Googe stresses the unformed appearance of this rock; the currency of wealth—precious metals and jewels—originate from the ground. Googe would have been familiar with this idea from Palingenius (*Zodiake* [1576], 89). Avarice, or *Avaritia,* is discussed in Chew, *Pilgrimage of Life*, 106–9.

St. 34 (l. 270): *rustie geare.* Moldy or unused material possessions (?).

St. 35 (l. 278): *hawtie.* High-minded, aspiring.

St. 36 (ll. 281–88): Googe here anticipates some of the imagery of Spenser's "Rich strond" in *FQ* 3.4. The passage also has similarities with the shipwreck encountered by Strephon and Klaius in Sidney's *Arcadia* 1.1.

St. 37 (ll. 289–96): The fears experienced by the man of wealth are described in Palingenius, *Zodiake* [1576], 21–22.

(l. 291): *wearish.* Feeble, wizened.

(l. 296): *poyse.* Weight, burden.

St. 38 (l. 302): *Cloyne.* Clown, country-fellow, simpleton.

(ll. 303–4): *For all is fish . . . net.* Proverbial, though not in Tilley. See, for example, Gascoigne, *The Steele Glas*, C3.

St. 40 (l. 314): *carke.* Distress, anxiety.

(ll. 318–20): *But takes them . . . sleepe.* Perhaps an allusion to the parable of the Rich Fool, Luke 12.16–21.

St. 41 (l. 323): *Oft wanting sleepe.* Palingenius treats of the rich man's insomnia (*Zodiake* [1576], 11).
(l. 326): *Plutoes raigne.* In Greek mythology, the realm of Hades, ruled by the god Pluto, often associated with Satan by Christian interpreters.
St. 43 (l. 340): *moyle.* Drudge, toil.
(l. 340): *Bayard.* Legendary bay-colored horse, taken as the type of blindness or blind recklessness.
St. 44 (ll. 345–52): The wickedness of Avarice is demonstrated by biblical illustration. This stanza is concerned with the parable popularly known as Dives and Lazarus (Luke 16.19–31).
(l. 345): *polde.* Pillaged, fleeced.
(l. 350): *him that preached.* Abraham. See Luke 16.24–31.
St. 45 (ll. 353–60): Based on the story of the Rich Young Ruler (Mark 10.17-31 and Luke 18.18–27).
St. 46 (l. 361): *factors.* Agents.
(l. 364): *usance.* Usury, interest.
St. 47 (ll. 369–76): Googe glances at a time-honored satiric theme, the corruption of lawyers.
(l. 374): *for to agree.* Happen to agree. The sense, here, is that the lawyer will fear to plead lest he too be charged by the Judge with avarice.
St. 48 (l. 379): *giltie gilted.* The guilty hand is perhaps gilded with rings or bracelets.
(l. 381): *throughly.* Thoroughly.
St. 49 (l. 385): *who sayleth.* Thou who saileth.
St. 50 (l. 399): *frankest.* Most honest.
(l. 400): *shrowde.* Shelter.
Sts. 51–52 (ll. 401–16): Googe translated Palingenius's preachments on *beneficentia* thus: "What thing more famous is than this? What more deserues the place / Of Gods aboue then for to helpe the poores afflicted case?" (*Zodiake* [1576], 22).
St. 53 (ll. 417–24): Next in the sequence of vices is the Quicksands of Detraction. The unpredictable and treacherous sands are an appropriate figure for the malicious. "The Booke to the reader" in the 1560 edition of Palingenius sees Googe likening his poetic endeavors to the passage of a ship through stormy seas: the buffets are the cynical comments of "scornefull tonges."
St. 56 (l. 443): *rid.* Variant of *ride.*
St. 58 (l. 459): *Their oares . . . barge.* Literally, putting their oar in.
(l. 460): *mell.* Meddle, interfere.
(l. 463): *looke . . . what.* Whatever.
St. 59 (l. 470): *momish.* Hypercritical, from Momus, the personification of fault-finding in Greek mythology.

St. 60 (l. 478): *Harpy.* In Greek mythology the daughters of Thaumus and Electra, having the form of large savage birds with the faces of women, are termed Harpies. One manifestation of their vicious behavior to which Googe refers is their habit of stealing or defecating on the food of others, as in Book 3 of Vergil's *Aeneid.* In Peacham's emblem *In repetundos, et adulatores,* false courtiers are likened to "a monstrous Harpie" that carries tales vntrue" (*Minerva Britanna,* 115). See Plate IV. Shakespeare refines the allegory further when Ariel appears "like a harpy" to the three men of sin in *The Tempest,* 3.3.

(l. 478): *file.* Defile.

St. 61 (ll. 481–88): The notion that detractors are akin to mobbing birds is enlarged upon in an emblem in Wither (*Collection of Emblemes,* 63).

St. 63 (ll. 497–504): Exodus tells how Moses's leadership of the Children of Israel from Egypt to Canaan was dogged by murmurings of discontent.

St. 65 (ll. 513–20): The story of Job's Comforters is to be found in Job 2–32.

St. 67 (l. 529): *That happy messenger:* John the Baptist.

(l. 536): *Reporteth . . . possest:* Matthew 11.18. Cf. Grey Brydges, Baron Chandos: "when Iohn Baptist came neither eating, nor drinking, they said hee had a Deuill. . . . And so forward, that there is almost nothing that a man can bee or doe, which a Detractor wil not peruert" (E3–E4v).

St. 68 (ll. 537–44): Matthew 11.19; Luke 7.34.

St. 69 (l. 545): *What should I.* Why should I. Also in st. 70 (l. 553).

St. 70 (l. 553): *cancred.* Envious, spiteful, ill-tempered.

(l. 553): *carlish.* Churlish.

(l. 556): *bewraye.* Betray, reveal, expose.

(l. 558): *wolvish.* Wolf-like. In addition to reducing slanderous remarks to the level of the savage or feral, Googe alludes to the widely made connection between the Roman Church and wolves. The idea was validated by certain readings of lupine references in the Bible and appeared to be confirmed by the story of Romulus and Remus, the founders of Rome, who, according to legend, had been nurtured by a she-wolf. The epithet "wolvish" is commonly applied to the Pope and Catholic clergy in the literature of the time: "For this reason . . . the Pope shold be of a woluish nature, because a wolfe was nurse to his first predecessor Romulus" (Taylor, *The Scvller Rowing,* C1). The identification was being made in England as early as 1529 in Simon Fish's *A Supplicacyon for the Beggars* (1). Chew lists some interesting associations of the wolf with Envy (*Pilgrimage of Life,* 109).

(l. 560): *seemes.* Beseems, befits.

St. 72 (l. 575): *Malebouche.* "Male Bouche" is a personification of slander and misreport in the *Roman de la Rose,* translated as "Wykked-Tonge" in the Chaucerian version (see ll. 3026–30, 3257–64, 3799–3820, 3870–80, 4141–44, 4233–76, and passim in the Robinson edition.

St. 74 (l. 592): *mo.* More.

St. 76 (ll. 601–6): *the gentle minde . . . majestie.* Man was created to be a microcosm of God upon earth.

(l. 607): *race.* Erase.

St. 77 (l. 614): *travaile.* Travel, as throughout, here with pun on travail, labor.

St. 78 (l. 617): *Hoyse.* Hoist.

(l. 620): *wey.* Weigh, consider.

St. 79 (l. 629): *sounding.* Measuring the water's depth.

St. 80 (ll. 633–40): The ship next encounters the Sandbanks of Gluttony. Gluttony, or *Gula,* is described in Chew, *Pilgrimage of Life,* 103–4.

St. 81 (ll. 641–42): It is appropriate that Googe gives the first mention to wine barrels, because one of the chief evils of Gluttony was excessive drinking. Spenser's representation of Gluttony makes special mention of his "bouzing can" (*FQ* 1.4.22).

(l. 644): *bankets.* Banquets, or perhaps banquettes, raised shelves at the back of a buffet.

St. 82 (l. 653): *them bie.* Beside them.

(l. 654): *As greedy lust can . . . .* As [many as] greedy lust can . . . .

St. 83 (l. 659): *groning gowte.* The painful inflammation of the joints in the foot, traditionally believed to be caused by a rich diet. In 1577 Googe was to translate a Latin verse treatise on the disease and dedicate it to the physician attending his kinsman and patron Sir William Cecil, who occasionally suffered from the disease. (See Ballista, *Overthrow of the Gout.*) Boorde's advice to the afflicted is to "fyrst reforme euyl dyet & surfetynge . . . and beware of drynkynge of wine" (Ff2).

(l. 661): *Dropsie.* Edema. Dropsy was particularly associated with excessive drinking. The disease afflicts Spenser's personification of Gluttony in *FQ* 1.4.21–23.

St. 84 (ll. 665–72): Googe describes a range of possible fevers awaiting the intemperate. They include "Quotidians" or intermittent fevers, "Quartans" or fevers that peak every fourth day, "double, halfe, and bastard Tertians" or various fevers that recur every three days, "continuars" or persistent fevers, and "Hecticke" or the fever associated with consumption.

(ll. 670–72): *Whereat Phisitions . . . helth.* A sentiment expressed in Palingenius: "By these same murdring knaues, / How many men both night and day haue found their fatall graues? / . . . It is not good therfore to truste such men, whose learning stands / In precious habits to be seene, and to adourne their hands / With rings and hoopes, and precious stones" (*Zodiake* [1576], 81).

St. 85 (l. 679): *falling sicknesse.* Epilepsy.

St. 86 (l. 683): *strangling quinsies.* Any growth, internal or external, that constricts the throat.

(l. 685): *Consuming Ptisicks.* Tuberculosis.

(l. 686): *Colics.* Abdominal pains.

(l. 687): *Stone.* Stones in the bladder were believed to have been caused by "eatyng of euyl and viscus meates & euyl drynkes, as thycke ale or beere, eatynge broyled or fryed meates, or meates yt be dryed in ye smoke as bacon, martynmas befe, reed herynge sprotes and salt meates, and crustes of breed, or of pasties and such lyke" (Boorde, *The Breuiary of Helthe*, X4).

(l. 687): *Strangurie.* Irregular and painful passage of urine.

St. 89 (l. 707): *farce.* Stuff.

(l. 712): *bumbast.* Stuffed.

St. 90 (ll. 713–20): The belief that Gluttony promoted lechery is familiar to us from the humorous soliloquy of Shakespeare's drunken Porter (*Macbeth* 2.3), but the theme was a commonplace in emblem books and iconologies: see, for example, de Bry, *Emblemata de Nobilitate*, 43: *Fallitvr et fallet Venvs insidiata tenebris*; Ripa, *Iconologia*, 50; Reusner, *Emblemata*, 31, *Quid Non Ebrietas Designat?*; and Whitney, *Choice of Emblemes*, 42. Both vices were evidence of immoderate appetite.

St. 94 (ll. 745–52): For another treatment by Googe of the virtuous abstemious, see *Eclogues*, ed. Kennedy, 55.

(l. 750): *Kites.* The bird was a type for greediness; see Alciato, *Latin Emblems*, 129; Palmer, *Emblems of Thomas Palmer*, 133; and Whitney, *Choice of Emblemes*, 170.

St. 95 (l. 757): *affections.* Sensual delights, as opposed to the government of reason.

St. 96 (l. 762): *Christ commaundeth so.* Christ does not explicitly advocate fasting in the Gospels, but endorses the practice in Matthew 17.21 and Mark 9.29.

(l. 763): *Our fathers olde.* The Fathers of the Primitive Church.

St. 98 (l. 777): *of.* Off.

Sts. 99–139 (ll. 785–1113): The section concerned with the Island of Fleshly Pleasure is the most detailed and sustained passage in the poem. Googe's treatment of *Luxuria* contains some memorable and euphonic writing allied to a certain conservatism of style: as well as the models of antiquity, Googe is heavily reliant upon the spirit of late medieval allegory. His treatment of the theme is of chief interest, though, as an anticipation of the direction Spenser was to take in his account of the Bower of Bliss (*FQ* 2.12).

St. 99 (ll. 790–92): *The sight . . . finde.* Googe points out the peculiarly alluring quality of this vice and the insidious dangers it poses.

St. 100 (ll. 797–800): *From whence . . . resound.* The fragrant and melodious air's sweet assault upon the senses of the mariner points towards the sexual enticements he will presently encounter.

(l. 798): *Amber Grece.* Ambergris was a prized ingredient in the manufacture of perfumes. A secretion from the intestines of sperm whales, it was found floating in tropical seas.

St. 101 (ll. 801–8): This passage bears resemblance to many well known *loci amoeni,* for example Spenser's Mount Acidale (*FQ* 6.10) and Belphoebe's pleasant glade (*FQ* 3.5), but perhaps Googe had in mind Palingenius's description of the environs of Lady Voluptuousnesse's Castle (*Zodiake* [1576], 28–31). In the marginalia to his translation, Googe makes explicit the allegorical implications of the *loftie Lordlye Pine.* He cites the story of Cybele and Attis, where the latter was metamorphosed into a pine tree after castrating himself in a frenzy of frustrated love. The myrtle was traditionally associated with the festival of Venus, as it was behind such a tree that the goddess sought cover when surprised bathing by wanton satyrs (Ovid, *Fasti* 4, 138ff.). Botticelli's great allegorical painting *Venus & Mars* in The National Gallery, London, depicts the two deities secluded in a myrtle grove. The *groves of Mirtels comly to be seene* anticipate Spenser's myrtle grove in *FQ* 3.6.43, and the catalog of trees that "thither draw the saylers wandring minde" (st. 102) resembles Spenser's more extensive arboretum in the Wandering Wood of *FQ* 1.1.8–10.

(l. 801): *Clives.* Cliffs.

St. 105 (l. 834): *shalls of Mermayds.* Shoals. The beautiful and melodious mermaids correspond to the Sirens in Homer, *Odyssey*, Book 12, ll. 39–54, 165–200. Mermaids beset Guyon in *FQ* 2.12.17, 30–33. Googe may have known Alciato's emblem *Sirenes* (*Latin Emblems,* 116), which warns of the evil end awaiting those who succumb to fleshly desire. See Plate V. A later emblem writer, H. G., was to use the sirens' song as a metaphor for the allure of the Church of Rome. See H. G., *Mirrovr of Maiestie,* 23.

St. 106 (ll. 841–48): The moralizing of Homer was standard in the Renaissance. The authoritative de Sponde edition of Homer printed in Basle in 1583, for example, was accompanied by detailed moral glosses.

St. 108 (l. 864): *amayne.* Amain, vehemently.

St. 110 (l. 878): *That.* Who, referring to the possessive "saylers" in the previous line.

St. 111 (l. 885): *fine garlands.* In Palingenius, the figure of Epicure wears a "flowry garland gay" as a badge of his wantonness and salacity (*Zodiake* [1576], 24).

St. 112 (l. 889): *roche.* Rock.

(l. 893): *set their hart a broche.* Pierce and stir their heart.

(l. 895): *hoyse and hale.* Originally the supposed noises made by sailors when pulling ropes, etc., here the action of the sailors changing tack.

St. 113 (l. 903): *light.* Disembark.

St. 114 (ll. 906–7): The nakedness and blindness of the sailors represent their thraldom and servitude to fleshly desires.

St. 115 (l. 913): *sumptuous Queene.* Her resemblance to Circe was first noted by Peirce ("Barnabe Googe: Poet and Translator," 193).

(l. 915): *caytifes.* Caitiffs, prisoners; also, base persons. Their baseness is due to their abandonment of reason for the pleasures of the flesh.

St. 117 (ll. 929–36): The sufferings detailed here are based on those accorded to Prometheus in punishment for his theft of fire from the gods. Typically, Prometheus's heart is continuously gnawed by an eagle; Googe's preferred *Kites and Pies and Ravens wood* (all birds that sometimes feed on carrion) allow him to stress the mortal perils attendant on unguarded appetite. Googe may be punning as well: "Kites" approximates to "cates" (delicacies), "Pies" (magpies) to the foodstuff, and "raven" is etymologically related to "ravenous." For another application of the Prometheus trope, see Alciato, *Latin Emblems*, 103 and Whitney, *Choice of Emblemes*, 75.

(l. 934): *leese.* Lose, cease.

St. 119 (ll. 945–52): The sailors' transformation into beasts reflects Circe's spell where her victims were changed to swine. Valeriano records that the association of swine with sexual excess was made by the ancient Egyptians (*Hieroglyphica*, 85–86). Palingenius records how "that Hag, dame Circes did transforme to swinish kinde / Vlysses mates." She also has the power to make men a "Lion, bore or bull, / Or made a Dogge, or else a Wolfe, the common plague to Sheepe" (*Zodiake* [1576], 34). Once more, the symbolism all points to the bestial nature of those driven by lubricious desire.

St. 120 (l. 955): *all their sayles clapped on.* Under full sail.

St. 122 (l. 969): *mightie Hercules.* The story of Hercules's subjugation to Circe is rehearsed in Palingenius, *Zodiake* [1576], 33–34, where Googe's marginal note reads, "The slauish subiection of Hercules being in Loue." Googe may also be alluding to the story of Hercules and Omphale, Queen of Lydia, who dressed Hercules in women's clothing and set him to domestic tasks.

St. 123 (ll. 977–84): *The subtill wit . . . ran.* The reference is probably to

Socrates, who, as Palingenius notes (*Zodiake* [1576], 5), was famously praised for wisdom by the oracle and whose marriage difficulties were legendary—see Chaucer, Wife of Bath's Prologue (Robinson ed. 83, III [D] 727–32) and Chaucer's source, Jerome's *Adversus Jovi-niam* (*Jankyn's Book* 82, 176–77). In Chaucer, as in Googe, Hercules is mentioned in the immediately preceding lines.

St. 124 (ll. 991–92): *Example . . . astray.* Googe refers to the story of David and Bathsheba in 2 Samuel 11 and 1 Kings 11. David's son, Solomon, offended God by his addiction to Gentile wives and concubines.

(l 991): *Uries wife.* Bathsheba was the wife of the Hittite Uriah.

St. 131 (l. 1045): *teene.* Misery, affliction.

St. 132 (l. 1052): *traine.* Lead, entice, lure.

St. 136 (l. 1082): *race.* Life.

St. 139 (ll. 1105–13): An anomalous nine-line stanza (abababacc). Cf. st. 179.

St. 140 (ll. 1114–21): Googe leaves fleshly temptations behind and focuses on spiritual dangers. The first of these is Heresy, figured as a half-submerged rock. The exposed rock is the credible front that false doctrine presents to the credulous while the great bulk of error remains out of view.

St. 144 (l. 1152): *drent.* Drenched, drowned. It is tempting to think that Googe alludes to the saving of the Church through the Reformation.

St. 145 (l. 1159): *him so dearely cost.* I.e., the Crucifixion.

St. 146 (l. 1163): *earst.* Formerly, with a possible pun on "errest."

(l. 1165): *devise.* Plan, contrivance.

(l. 1169): *As . . . shame.* As since [they did] the world has resounded with [the] shame [of it].

St. 147 (ll. 1170–77): Googe catalogs a series of early Church teachers condemned for heterodoxy: Cerinthus (fl. c.100), a Gnostic of Asia Minor; Eutyches (c.378–c.452), archimandrite of Constantinople; Novatus, or Novatian (d. 257–258), rigorist Bishop of Rome; Nestorius (d. 451?), patriarch of Constantinople; Arius (c.256–336), Libyan theologian; and the Manichees, followers of Manichaeanism, a religion founded by Mani, of Baghdad (c.216–c.276).

St. 150 (ll. 1200–1): The insistence that all religious teaching should be measured against scriptural authority is an overtly Protestant tenet.

St. 151 (l. 1202): *prating sprite.* A type for bogus religious teachers (*prating:* chattering on to little purpose).

(l. 1206): *Of these . . . light.* Googe refers to a biblical text often used by reformers to enforce the primacy of the Scriptures: "thy word is a lamp unto my feet, and a light unto my path" (Psalm 119, 105).

St. 153 (l. 1218): For a discussion of the identity of this unnamed individual, see the Introduction, pp. xxxi–xxxii.

(l. 1220): *tittell.* Tiniest detail, whit.

(l. 1220): *straight.* Strict.

St. 155 (ll. 1234–41): Arius, the originator of the the Arian heresy, was in the popular tradition responsible for violent outrages upon true believers. (See "Arianism" in *The New Encyclopaedia Britannica*, 549–50.) Googe's reference to religious persecution is a veiled comment on Inquisition practices.

St. 157 (l. 1250): *Chrysostome.* St. John Chrysostom, fourth-century Bishop of Constantinople, was highly esteemed by the reformers for his outspoken attacks upon greed and pretension, and for his advocacy of strict biblical principles. In 1570, Googe described him as "full of holiness, / Whose wordes doe like a fountaine flowe, and eke whose worthie wit / For eloquence excelles, amid whose lappes doth Pitho sit" (Naogeorgus, *Popish Kingdome*, Bb3^v).

(l. 1251): *brittell.* Unstable, transitory.

St. 158 (ll. 1258–61): *Did ever yet . . . hunting them.* The extension of the Rome-wolf notion to the Romish wolf preying on the sheep of Christ's flock proved irresistible to many reformers.

(ll. 1261–63): *So Cain . . . Isaac him.* The dangers of schism are illustrated by biblical types, the internecine jealousies of Cain and Abel (Genesis 4) and Isaac and Ishmael (Genesis 21–25).

St. 159 (l. 1269): *still.* Always.

(l. 1270): *To be the wolves . . . tolde.* Cf. Matthew 7.15, Matthew 10.16, and Luke 10.3.

Sts. 161–80 (ll. 1282–1442): The next spiritual hazard to be encountered is Idolatry, figured as an island. Protestant sensibilities were offended by the Roman Catholic enthusiasm for statues, shrines, and ecclesiastical ornament, all of which reformers deemed idolatrous.

St. 162 (l. 1290): *Pyramides.* Googe chooses pyramids as an instantly recognizable badge of the false gods worshipped by the heathen races in the Old Testament. Pyramids are associated with astrology and sophistry in Valeriano (*Hieroglyphica*, 640). There is also an echo of the Tower of Babel story, where humans presumed to build a tower that would reach to heaven (Genesis 11.4–9).

(l. 1296): *Adourned brave . . . light.* The false light of the torches seeks to obscure the true light of the sun.

St. 163 (ll. 1298–1305): The dressing of altars and the use of censers was frowned upon by reformers. See Naogeorgus, *Popish Kingdome*, F1^v.

Sts. 164–65 (ll. 1306–21): The inventory of gods and goddesses from the classical pantheon equates the Roman Catholic penchant for images with paganism. The inclusion of Asclepius in the list may be of significance, because he was often presented as a false Christ who could heal the body but not the soul; see Spenser (*FQ*, 1.5.36–40). The snakes, his traditional attribute, refer to the caduceus of medical learning and the creatures associated with his cult at Epidaurus, but hint at poison, death, and Original Sin.

St. 165 (l. 1318): *Berecynthya.* Cybele.

St. 166 (l. 1325): *As one that portred is with faces three.* The trifrontal figure is Hecate, goddess of witchcraft. Her three faces are traditionally those of a dog, a horse, and a boar. See Valeriano, *Hieroglyphica,* 629. "Triple Hecate" is mentioned in *A Midsummer Night's Dream* 5.2.

(l. 1326): *An other . . . speare.* St. George, patron saint of England. Googe addresses him elsewhere as "valiant George with speare thou killest the dreadfull dragon here" (Naogeorgus, *Popish Kingdome,* Q1^{v}).

(ll. 1327–29): *Another holding . . . hie.* St. Christopher, patron saint of travellers. Like St. George, St. Christopher was popular in England. Googe's attack on them demonstrates the new distaste among reformers for the veneration of the saints so widespread in the old faith.

St. 167 (ll. 1330–37): The identity of this androgynous saint is obscure, but it could be a representation of the papacy itself. The *Lettice cap* was a type of tricorn hat made of fur, popularly supposed to induce sleep. The three peaks could be an allusion to the pope's triple tiara; certainly Stubbes makes the connection: "some weare Lattice cappes with three hornes, three corners I shuld saie, like the forked cappes of Popishe Priestes" (*Anatomie of Abuses,* 69). The reference to the figure's liking for oats may be a reference to the Lutheran identification of the Pope with an ass.

(l. 1333): *beare a port.* Bear a resemblance.

(l. 1336): *masking Cotes.* Suggestive of its duplicity; perhaps also a reference to players' apparel, distasteful to the Puritan mind.

St. 168 (ll. 1338–45): In listing the images of Islamic figures, Googe seems to be ignorant of the Muslim proscription of representing Creation in visual art.

(l. 1342): *Meschyts.* Mosques (variant of *mesquita*).

(ll. 1344–45): Googe's source for the Muslim "saints" he lists is not known. "Chidirell the king" may be related to the deity Johann Weyer called in his *De praestigiis daemonum* of 1583 "Chiridirelles," who "customarily helps travelers in need. They say that he appears to those who call upon him in the form of a traveller, sitting upon a horse" (17). The name is given as "Chidrelles" and respelled "Khidr" by F. W. Hasluck in *Christianity and Islam under the Sultans* (1929), 790, 822–23.

St. 170 (l. 1360): *despite.* Spite, contempt, outrage.

(l. 1361): *That this detests . . . thing.* Because of the warning against idolatry in the first of the Ten Commandments; see Exodus 20.

St. 173 (ll. 1379–85): *His chosen flocke . . . will.* The Children of Israel's lapses into idolatry and their establishing of shrines in groves and high places is a theme that runs throughout the Old Testament. See, for example, Deuteronomy 12.2, Judges 6.25, Numbers 22.41, 2 Kings 17.9, and 2 Chronicles 11.15.

St. 176 (ll. 1403–5): *Let Paule . . . ease.* The Pauline injunction is located at 1 Corinthians 10.14–21.

Sts. 178–79 (ll. 1418–34): Googe turns from the conspicuous worship of idols to spiritual idolatry, where the object of too great esteem may be a loved one. This warning to the devotee and the uxorious urges the primacy of God's demands upon our affections.

St. 179 (ll. 1426–34): Anomalous nine-line stanza. Cf. st. 139.

(l. 1431): *As . . . teach.* As those [acknowledge] who are instructed by the love of God.

St. 181 (ll. 1443–50): After Heresy comes the fair-seeming hazard of Hypocrisy.

Interpolation (ll. 1467–1502): The passage is taken from *The Romaunt of the Rose* 413–48. The source text used by Googe was Thynne's edition of 1532. Googe's abdication of authorial voice may seem strange if we forget the continued esteem in which Chaucer was held in Elizabethan times. Webbe regarded Chaucer as the "God of English Poets" and stressed his role as the scourge of the hypocrite thus: "by his delightsome vayne, [he] so gulled the eares of men with his deuises, that, although corruption bare such sway in most matters, that learning and truth might skant bee admitted to shewe it selfe, yet without controllment, myght hee gyrde at the vices and abuses of all states, and gawle with very sharpe and eger inuentions, which he did so learnedly and pleasantly, that none therefore would call him into question. For such was his bolde spirit, that what enormities he saw in any, he would not spare to pay them home, eyther in playne words, or els in some prety and pleasant couert, that the simplest might espy him" (32). Chaucer's appeal can be explained by a matrix of reasons, most importantly that his decision to write in English was highly significant for mid-Tudor versifiers, and his strident anticlericism qualified him as something of a proto-Protestant. See King, *English Reformation Literature*, 50–52, and King, *Spenser's Poetry*, 20–27.

Interpolation (l. 1467): *done their write.* Written down there.

Interpolation (l. 1469): *Pope holye.* According to F. N. Robinson's note on l. 415 of the Chaucerian *Romaunt* (*The Works of Geoffrey Chaucer*, 873–74), the term means *hypocritical,* from the French "papelardie." "The original meaning of 'papelard' appears to have been 'glutton' (from Fr. 'paper,' eat, and 'lard,' bacon). The English form 'pope-holy' is due to popular etymology."

Interpolation (l. 1483): *Youlden.* Yielded, given over.

Interpolation (l. 1486): *fonde.* Try, endeavor.

Interpolation (ll. 1490–91): *intentiffe / To:* intent on, bent upon.

Interpolation (l. 1492): *haire.* Hair-shirt.

Interpolation (l. 1502): *lesen.* Lose.

St. 184 (l. 1504): *descrived.* Described in writing.

St. 185 (l. 1518): *blear.* Blind, mislead.

St. 187 (l. 1529): *huckermucker.* Huggermugger, clandestinely, secretly. A common Tudor word, it could also be rendered *hugger mugger,* as in Spenser's *Mother Hubberds Tale,* l. 139.

St. 188 (ll. 1535–42): Based on Matthew 23.13–14.

St. 190 (l. 1555): *lust.* Will.

St. 192 (l. 1567): *visard.* Mask. The mask is a common attribute in hypocrite types; see, for example, the figures of Fraud in Joannes David, *Veridicus christianus* (145), and Vice in Wither (*Collection of Emblemes,* 22). Masks represent deceit in Thomas Combe, *The Theater of Fine Devices* ($B1^v$).

(ll. 1571–74): *The Purple garments . . . spide.* A vigorous rehearsal of the Erasmian adage "an ape is always an ape even if clad in purple" (Erasmus 88). The ape is the type for hypocrisy in John Davies of Hereford's *Wittes Pilgrimage,* Sonnet 40.

St. 194 (ll. 1583–84): *Now veer . . . abroade.* Having successfully negotiated the moral and spiritual dangers, the ship of the soul can unfurl (*veer*) its sails and proceed with confidence.

(l. 1586): *roade.* An open area where ships may safely drop anchor.

St. 197 (l. 1608): *blasphemie.* Stubbes considered it preferable for "one to kill a man . . . then to sweare an othe" (*Anatomie of Abuses,* 133).

Sts. 198–99 (ll. 1615–30): *Carlish* (churlish, boorish) *crueltie* and *hatred* approximate to the traditional Cardinal Sin of Wrath, or *Ira.*

St. 199 (l. 1625): *suttle.* Subtle, careful, conscientious.

St. 200 (l. 1631): *embrued.* Stained, steeped.

(ll. 1633–36): *On top . . . light.* Fury shaking his sword resembles traditional representations of Wrath. See Chew, *Pilgrimage of Life,* 112.

(l. 1637): *The Fiend himselfe.* Satan.

St. 201 (l. 1646): *oken ancour.* An emblem of their precarious condition, as a wooden anchor is useless. The anchor was the universal badge of Hope, after the usage in Hebrews 6.19. This ineffectual anchor points up the hopelessness of those addicted to theft and robbery.

St. 202 (l. 1651): *infidelitie.* Atheism. Googe had translated Palingenius's discussion of atheism. See *Zodiake* [1576], 145.

St. 202 (l. 1654): *randon.* Random.

St. 203 (ll. 1655–62): Googe targets a range of miscreants: the prognosticators, almanac writers, and adherents of divination. The 1560s had witnessed an unprecedented upsurge in apocalyptic literature; see Wilson, *Signs and Portents*, 40–49.

(l. 1661): *cunning men.* The wise men of a community, often versed in herbal and meteorological lore. There is also a possible pun on "conning."

(l. 1662): *While as . . . pen.* The writers of spurious prophecies regularly peddled their material under the name of long-dead, but respected, authorities who, as Keith Thomas has said, "were in no position to deny their authenticity" (*Religion and the Decline of Magic*, 464). Either Googe himself or his son and namesake was to suffer his name being associated with such a publication in 1672, when an enigmatic pamphlet on Anglo-Dutch relations was attributed to "Doctor Barnaby Googe that Lived in the Reign of Qu. Elizabeth."

Sts. 204–6 (ll. 1663–86): Googe counsels the reader to hold a moderate hope of heaven, allowing neither Presumption nor Desperation to lead to error. Desperation may include the mortal sin of suicide.

St. 206 (l. 1686): *warely.* Warily.

St. 209 (ll. 1703–10): 1 Thessalonians 5.5–17.

St. 210 (l. 1716): *sound.* Test the water's depth.

St. 211 (ll. 1719–26): The personification of Love is particularly vague here. Love takes the shape of a woman, but whether she stands on shore or on the waves is unclear. The allegory is, at best, desultory in this closing section.

St. 212 (ll. 1727–34): Matthew 18.21–35.

St. 215 (ll. 1751–58): Perhaps conscious of his earlier preachments on Heresy, Googe claims that his theology follows a time-honored tradition.

St. 216 (l. 1765): *where.* Whereas.

Sts. 217–18 (ll. 1767–82): Googe observes the reformist decorum of not representing the glories of heaven in a physical form. The tenet was partly a reaction against the Popish taste for images of God, Christ, the saints, etc., and partly a sense of artistic inadequacy in the face of such ineffable wonders. When one of the Jesuit source plates of Quarles's *Emblemes* disobligingly showed an open heaven with God and the company of angels in glory, the poet felt it necessary to ask the reader to "Excuse my bold attempt, and pardon me / For shewing Sense, what Faith alone should see" (297).

St. 217 (l. 1774): *blasde.* Blazoned, illustrated.

St. 218 (ll. 1781–82): *No eye . . . preparde.* Cf. 1 Cor. 2:9.

St. 219 (ll. 1783–90): The poem closes with an exhortation bidding the reader to seek God's grace, adhere to Christ's teachings, and follow the godly life with vigor.

"The death of S. Polycarpus"

Googe found his source for this tale in the Latin translation of the *Ecclesiastical History* of Eusebius made by Tyrannius Rufinus of Aquileia around 401 A.D. We have consulted a photocopy of *Ecclesiastica Historia diui Eusebii: et Ecclesiastica historia gentis anglorum venerabilis Bede* (Strassburg: George Husner, 1500), but in quoting we follow the modernized orthography of the edition of Rufinus by Theodore Mommsen in Eusebius, *Kirchengeschichte,* edited by Eduard Schwartz, 3 vols., cont. pag. (Leipzig: J. C. Hinrichs, 1903–9), hereinafter cited as Rufinus, and Eusebius, *Ecclesiastical History,* Vol. 1, translated by Kirsopp Lake, Loeb Classical Library (London: Heinemann, 1926), hereinafter cited as Eusebius.

Ll. 1–14: The opening fourteen lines are not to be found in Eusebius or Rufinus, whose translation of the Polycarp episode closely follows the Greek, but are rather Googe's own. They serve as an induction to the action of Eusebius's account of Polycarp's martyrdom. See Eusebius, 343–57, and Rufinus, 339–53.

L. 1: *Alecto.* One of the Furies, whose name means unceasing (in pursuit).

Ll. 5–6: *The poore . . . dide.* Googe insinuates a contemporary application.

L. 13: *spials.* Spies.

L. 14: *suite.* Pursuit.

L. 16: Line added by Googe. See Eusebius, 343; Rufinus, 339.

L. 24: Explanatory elaboration added by Googe. See Eusebius, 345; Rufinus, 339.

Ll. 26–28: Elaboration by Googe. See Eusebius, 345; Rufinus, 339–41.

L. 28: *In little . . . then.* In a short time, as it seemed to him in the dream.

L. 32: *leave his aged limmes.* Added by Googe. See Eusebius, 345; Rufinus, 341.

L. 35: *the tyrants foote.* Googe thus abbreviates a passage describing the bishop's new hiding place. See Eusebius, 345; Rufinus, 341.

L. 38: *Sathans cursed brood.* Added by Googe. See Eusebius, 345; Rufinus, 341.

L. 41: *Catchpolles.* Arresting officers, literally, those who caught a fugitive by the "poll," head, or hair. "Cursed Catchpolles" is Googe's elaboration. Ll. 39–44 are considerably expanded from the source, and Googe omits Polycarp's quoted refusal to attempt another escape: "The Lord's will be done"; "voluntas domini fiat." See Eusebius, 345; Rufinus, 341.

Ll. 50–58: This extended recommendation of Christian fortitude in the face of persecution is Googe's own. See Eusebius, 345; Rufinus, 341.

L. 58: *amase.* Perplex, terrify.

L. 60: *ghestly.* Guestly. Polycarpus is treating his captors as if they were his guests by sitting them down for dinner while he goes to pray.

L. 62: *he falleth . . . his face.* Added by Googe. See Eusebius, 345; Rufinus, 341.

L. 66: *tho.* then.

Ll. 69: Here, Googe omits a passage stating that Polycarp prayed for the whole Catholic Church. See Eusebius, 347; Rufinus, 341–43.

L. 78: *calling of the Emperor God.* Googe thus clarifies a passage literally translated "to say Lord Caesar" (Eusebius, 347); "dicere dominum Caesarem" (Rufinus, 343).

Ll. 79–83: Added by Googe, thus dramatizing the temptation of spiritual compromise. See Eusebius, 347; Rufinus, 343.

Ll. 85–86: Added by Googe. See Eusebius, 347; Rufinus, 343.

Ll. 88–89: Intensified by Googe; cf. Eusebius, 347: "turned him out in such a hurry that in getting down from the wagon he scraped his shin"; Rufinus, 343: "indignatione commoti cum contumelia eum vehiculo deturbant, ita ut pedem laederet praeceps actus."

L. 92: Googe explains what the source refers to as "a great uproar in the arena" (Eusebius, 347); "vero tumultus ingens in stadio" (Rufinus, 343).

L. 94: Googe changes the emphasis to purely religious exhortation from "Be strong, Polycarp, and play the man" in Eusebius (347), "fortis esto, Polycarpe, et viriliter age" in Rufinus (343).

Ll. 96–99: Passage considerably elaborated by Googe. See Eusebius, 347; Rufinus, 343.

L. 98: *defacing.* Defaming.

L. 100: Added by Googe. See Eusebius, 349; Rufinus 343.

L. 102: Googe converts source to direct discourse. See Eusebius, 349; Rufinus 343.

L. 105: *reverent.* Reverend.

L. 107: *all such beasts / as doe no God regarde.* Cf. Eusebius, 349, "the Atheists"; Rufinus, 345, "sacrilegos."

L. 108: *harde.* Heard.

L. 110: *such as God doe here despise.* Variation of line 107, whereas "sacrilegos" is repeated in Rufinus, 345.

L. 115: *my frende.* Cf. Eusebius, 349, "my King"; Rufinus, 345, "regem meum."

Ll. 117–20: Passage elaborated by Googe. See Eusebius, 349; Rufinus, 345.

L. 128: *so that.* As long as.

L. 133: *Shrife.* Sheriff, magistrate. Cf. Eusebius, 349, "proconsul"; Rufinus, 345, "proconsul."

L. 134: *lose.* Loose.

Ll. 135–36: *more meete this sinfull brood, / Should leave their lewde and beastly life.* Added by Googe. See Eusebius, 349; Rufinus, 345.

L. 136: *offended much / and boyling all in ire.* Added by Googe. See Eusebius, 349–51; Rufinus, 345.

L. 139: *werish.* Frail, feeble.

Ll. 139–40: Added by Googe. See Eusebius, 351; Rufinus, 345.

Ll. 145–46: *put beasts . . . moved be.* Added by Googe. See Eusebius, 351; Rufinus, 345.

L. 149: *Baily.* Bailiff. Cf. Eusebius, 351, "herald"; Rufinus, 347, "curione."

L. 150: *had thrice confest.* A mistranslation of Eusebius by Rufinus, perpetuated by Googe. In Eusebius, the herald makes his announcement three times, while in Rufinus and Googe, Polycarp is said to have confessed three times. See Eusebius, 351; Rufinus, 347.

L. 156: Googe omits a passage after this line in which the crowd clamors for a lion. See Eusebius, 351; Rufinus, 347.

L. 158: Googe is anxious to minimize the marvels attendant on Polycarp's martyrdom. Here, for example, he omits a passage recalling Polycarp's prophetic vision of fire. See Eusebius, 351; Rufinus 347.

L. 164: *staples.* Googe manifests his familiarity with sixteenth-century practice, for in the source, nails are used. See Eusebius, 353, "to nail him"; Rufinus, 347, "clavis ad figere." Googe just before omits a passage about how Polycarp was unused to taking off his own shoes because of the zeal of his followers to touch his flesh.

L. 170: *casting up . . . hands.* In the source, Polycarp's hands are tied. See Eusebius, 353; Rufinus, 349.

Ll. 171–92: Googe expands Polycarp's prayer, adding Protestant elements. Cf. Eusebius, 353–55; Rufinus, 349.

L. 196: *crooked compasse.* Bending encirclement.

L. 197: Googe omits a comment in the source that it is "a marvel," "miracula." See Eusebius, 355; Rufinus, 349.

L. 202: *hangman.* Eusebius, 355: "an executioner"; Rufinus, 349: "confectorem."

L. 205: *In divers places of the pile.* Googe minimizes the miraculous aspects of Polycarp's demise. Cf. Eusebius, 355: "the fire was quenched"; Rufinus, 349: "restingueret rogum."

Ll. 206–7: Googe adds a conclusion strikingly different from the source. Googe stresses that the body "neglected lies," whereas Eusebius goes on to describe how the martyr's bones were gathered up from the ashes and venerated as "more precious than precious stones, and finer than gold"; "pretiosissimus gemmis cariora et omni auro" (Eusebius, 357; Rufinus 353).

"A Priest of Apollo straungely converted"

This story was added to the church history by Rufinus, and it appears in his Book VII (Chapter 25, which corresponds to Chapter 28 in Eusebius) rather than Book IV as Googe's headnote wrongly states. See Rufinus, 953. The portion Googe translates appears on pages 954–55. Googe follows Rufinus closely but adds details of setting, action, and dialogue.

L. 2: *gorgeous temple faire.* Googe's elaboration, which may allude to the Protestant dislike of richly adorned Roman Catholic churches.
L. 11: *whereas.* Where.
L. 16: *Phebus.* Phoebus, i.e., Apollo.
L. 25: *Church.* I.e., the temple of Apollo. Rufinus uses *fanum* throughout.
L. 44: *slome.* Sloom, slumber.
L. 46: *ernfull.* Anxious.
L. 57: *my staye.* That I am blocked.
L. 65: *quire.* Choir, synecdoche for church or temple.
L. 72: *If . . . remaine.* If Apollo should thus remain silent.
Ll. 83–84: Added by Googe. See Rufinus, 955.
L. 89: *Idoll.* Rufinus, 955: "simulacrum."
Ll. 90–93: Added by Googe. See Rufinus, 955.

WORKS CONSULTED

Alciato, Andrea. *The Latin Emblems.* Edited and translated by Peter M. Daly, Virginia C. Callahan, and Simon Cuttler. Index Emblematicus, vol. 1. Toronto: University of Toronto Press, 1985.

Arber, Edward. "Notes on the Life and Writings of Barnabe Googe" and "Introduction." In Googe, Barnabe. *Eglogs, Epytaphes, and Sonnettes.* Edited by Arber. Pp. 5–18.

Aston, Margaret. *The King's Bedpost: Reformation and Iconography in a Tudor Group Portrait.* Cambridge: Cambridge University Press, 1993.

Auden, W. H. *The Enchafèd Flood, or the Romantic Iconography of the Sea.* New York: Random House, 1950.

Baldwin, William, *et al. The Mirror for Magistrates.* Edited by Lily B. Campbell. Cambridge: Cambridge University Press, 1938.

Ballista, Christopher. *The Overthrow of the Gout.* Translated by Barnabe Googe. Edited by Simon McKeown. London: Indelible Inc., 1990.

Barnett, Richard C. *Place, Profit and Power: A Study of the Servants of William Cecil, Elizabethan Statesman.* Chapel Hill: University of North Carolina Press, 1969.

Bateman, Stephen. *A christall glasse of christian reformation wherein the godly maye beholde the coloured abuses vsed in this our tyme.* London: John Day, 1569.

——. *The Trauayled Pylgrime, bringing newes from all partes of the worlde.* London: n.p., 1569.

Bath, Michael. *Speaking Pictures: English Emblem Books and Renaissance Culture.* London: Longman, 1994.

Beckingsale, Bernard W. *Burghley: Tudor Statesman, 1520–1598.* London: Macmillan, 1967.

Bertholdus, Andreas. *The Wonderfull and strange effect and vertues of a new Terra Sigillata lately found out in Germanie.* Translated by Barnabe Googe. London: Richard Robinson f. R. Watkins, 1587.

The holie bible. 2nd ed. London: Richard Jugge, 1572.

Blumenberg, Hans. *Shipwreck with Spectator: Paradigm of a Metaphor for Existence.* Translated by Steven Rendell. Cambridge, Mass.: MIT Press, 1997.

The Boke of common praier, and administration of the Sacramentes, and other rites and Ceremonies in the Churche of Englande. London: Richard Grafton, 1559.

Boorde, Andrew. *The Breuiary of Helthe (1547).* English Experience, 362. Amsterdam: Da Capo, 1970.

Borgiani, Guiseppi. *Marcello Palingenio e il suo poema lo* Zodiacus Vitae. Citta di Castello, 1912.

Brewer, Thomas. *Lord have mercy upon us. . . .* London: Henry Gosson, 1636.

Bruce, F. F. *The History of the Bible in English.* London: Lutterworth, 1970.

Bry, Theodore de. *Emblemata de Nobilitate et Officio Heraldico.* Frankfurt: de Bry, 1592.

Brydges, Grey, Baron Chandos. *Horae subseciuae: observations and discourses.* London: Edward Blount, 1620. Repr. as *Observations and Discourses.* New York: Da Capo Press, 1970.

Brydges, Samuel Egerton, and Joseph Haslewood. *The British Bibliographer.* 4 vols. London: R. Triphook, 1810–14.

Bunyan, John. *The Pilgrim's Progress From This world To That which is to come (1678 & 1684).* London: Ducimus, 1975.

Burroughs, Jeremiah. *The sea mans direction in time of storme.* London: T. Paine and M. Simmons, 1640.

Bush, Douglas. *Mythology and the Renaissance Tradition in English Poetry.* Minneapolis: University of Minnesota Press, 1932.

[Cabasilas], Nilus. *A Brief Treatise, Conteynynge a playne and fruitfull declaration of the Popes vsurped Primacye.* Translated by Thomas Gressop. London: H. Sutton f. Ralph Newbury, 1560.

Cebes' Tablet: Facsimiles of the Greek Text and Selected Translations. Edited by Sandra Sider. New York: The Renaissance Society of America, 1979.

Chambers, R. *The Book of Days: A Miscellany of Popular Antiquities.* 2 vols. London & Edinburgh: W. & R. Chambers, 1863–64.

Chaucer, Geoffrey. *The Riverside Chaucer.* 3rd ed. Edited by Larry D. Benson. Oxford: Oxford University Press, 1988.

——. *The Works, 1532, with Supplementary Material from the Editions of 1542, 1561, 1598, and 1602.* Edited by D. S. Brewer. Ilkely, Yorks.: Scolar, 1969.

——. *The Works of Geoffrey Chaucer.* 2nd ed. Edited by F. N. Robinson. Boston: Houghton Mifflin and Company, Inc., 1957.

Chew, Samuel C. *The Pilgrimage of Life.* New Haven: Yale University Press, 1962.

Chrysostom, St. John, Bishop of Neocaesarea. *Homilae duae.* Translated by John Cheke. London: R. Wolfe, 1543.

——. *Theorremon.* Translated by John Willovghbie. Oxford: Joseph Barnes, 1602.
——. *On the Incomprehensible Nature of God.* Translated by Paul W. Harkins. Vol. 72, The Fathers of the Church. Washington, D.C.: Catholic University of America Press, 1984.
——. *Homilies on Genesis.* Translated by Robert C. Hill. Vol. 82, The Fathers of the Church. Washington, D.C.: Catholic University of America Press, 1990.
Cockcroft, Robert. *The Voyage of Life: Ship Imagery in Art, Literature and Life.* Nottingham: University of Nottingham Press, 1982.
Collier, J. Payne. *A Bibliographical and Critical Account of the Rarest Books in the English Language.* 4 vols. New York: David G. Francis and Charles Scribner, 1866.
——. *Poetical Decameron.* 2 vols. Edinburgh: Archibald Constable, 1820.
Combe, Thomas. *The Theater of Fine Devices (1593? & 1614).* Introduction by Mary V. Silcox. Aldershot: Scolar, 1990.
Cradocke, Edward. *The shippe of assured safetie.* London: William Norton, 1572.
D., T. H. *Nine Rockes to Avoided of those which sayle towards the Port of Perfection.* Douai: Frauncis Fouler, 1600.
David, Johannes. *Veridicus christianus.* Antwerp: Christopher Plantin, 1601.
Davies of Hereford, John. *Wittes Pilgrimage.* London, 1605.
The Dictionary of National Biography. Edited by Leslie Stephen and Sidney Lee. Vol. 22. London: Smith, Elder & Co., 1885–1900.
Eccles, Mark. "Barnabe Googe in England, Spain, and Ireland." *English Literary Renaissance* 15 (1985): 353–70.
Edwards, Philip. *Sea-Mark: The Metaphorical Voyage, Spenser to Milton.* Liverpool English Texts & Studies 30. Liverpool: University of Liverpool Press, 1997.
Elslyot, Thomas. *The true mariner and his pixis nautical.* London: s.n., 1652.
Erasmus, Desiderius. *Praise of Folly.* Edited and translated by Betty Radice. London: Penguin, 1971.
Eusebius. *Ecclesiastica Historia diui Eusebii.* Translated by Tyrannius Rufinus. In *Ecclesiastica Historia diui Eusebii: et Ecclesiastica historia gentis anglorum venerabilis Bede.* Strassburg: George Husner, 1500.
——. *Ecclesiastical History.* Vol. 1. Translated by Kirsopp Lake. Loeb Classical Library. London: Heinemann, 1926. 2 vols.
——. *The History of the Church.* Translated by G. A. Williamson. London: Penguin, 1989.
——. *Kirchengeschichte.* 3 vols., cont. pag. Greek with Latin translation by Tyrannius Rufinus. Edited by Eduard Schwartz and Theodor Mommsen. Leipzig: J. C. Hinrichs, 1903–9.
Fish, Simon. *A Supplicacyon for the Beggars.* [England]: N.p., N.d.

Fox, Robin Lane. *Pagans and Christians.* Harmondsworth: Viking, 1986.
G., H. *The Mirrovr of Maiestie, or the Badges of Honovr Conceitedly Emblazoned.* 1618. Repr. edited by Henry Green and James Croston. The Holbein Society. London and Manchester: A. Brothers & Trübner & Co., 1870.
Gascoigne, George. *The Steele Glas.* London: Richard Smith, 1576.
Gent, Lucy, and Nigel Llewellyn, eds. *Renaissance Bodies: The Human Figure in English Culture c. 1540–1660.* London: Reaktion, 1990.
Googe, Barnabe. *Eclogues, Epitaphs and Sonnets.* Edited by Judith M. Kennedy. Toronto: University of Toronto Press, 1989.
——. *Eglogs, Epytaphes, and Sonettes.* London: Thomas Colwell f. Ralph Newbury, 1563.
——. *Eglogs, Epytaphes, and Sonettes.* Edited by Edward Arber. English Reprints. London: E. Arber, 1871.
Googe, Barnaby, D. D. (attributed author). *A Prophecie Lately Transcribed From an Old Manuscript of Doctor Barnaby Googe That Lived in the Reign of Qu. Elizabeth Predicting The Rising, Meridian, and Falling condition Of the States of the United Provinces.* London: B. L., 1672.
Hasluck, F. W. *Christianity and Islam under the Sultans.* 2 vols., cont. pag. 1929. Repr. New York: Octagon, 1973.
Heresbach, Conrad. *Fovre Bookes of Husbandry.* Translated by Barnabe Googe. London: Richard Watkins, 1577.
——. *The Whole Art of Husbandry.* Translated by Barnabe Googe. Revised by Gervase Markham. London: T. C. f. Richard More, 1631.
Heresbachius, Conrad. *Foure Bookes of Husbandry (1577).* Translated by Barnabe Googe. English Experience, 323. Amsterdam: Da Capo Press, 1973.
Homer. *Homeri quae extant omnia.* Edited by J. de Sponde. Basle: S. Episcopus, 1583.
——. *Chapman's Homer.* Translated by George Chapman. Edited by Allardyce Nicoll. 2nd ed. 2 vols. Bollingen Ser. 41. Princeton: Princeton University Press, 1967.
——. *The Odyssey.* Translated and edited by Albert Cook. New York: Norton, 1974.
Hughes, Philip Edgcumbe. *The Theology of the English Reformers.* London: Hodder and Stoughton, 1965.
Hull, John. *The Arte of christian saylinge.* London: J. Harrison & S. Stafford f. J. Harison, 1602.
Hussey, Christopher. *Scotney Castle.* London: National Trust, 1990.
Hussey, Edward. "Scotney Castle." *Archaeologia Cantiana* 17 (1887): 38–48.
Jankyn's Book of Wikked Wyves: Volume 1: The Primary Texts. Edited by Ralph Hanna III and Traugott Lawler. Athens: University of Georgia Press, 1997.
Jerome, Saint. *Adversus Jovinianm.* In *Jankyn's Book . . .*, 157–93.

Kane, Sean. *Spenser's Moral Allegory*. Toronto: University of Toronto Press, 1989.

Kennedy, Judith M. "Barnabe Googe." *Dictionary of Literary Biography. Volume 132: Sixteenth-Century British Nondramatic Writers First Series*. Detroit: Gale Research, 1994. 141–48.

——. "Googe, Barnabe." *The Spenser Encyclopedia*. Edited by A. C. Hamilton et al., 336–37. Toronto: University of Toronto Press, 1990, 1997.

King, John N. *English Reformation Literature: The Tudor Origins of the Protestant Tradition*. Princeton: Princeton University Press, 1982.

——. *Spenser's Poetry and the Reformation Tradition*. Princeton, N.J.: Princeton University Press, 1990.

Kirchmeyer. *See* Naogeorgus, Thomas.

Kolve, V. A. *Chaucer and the Imagery of Narrative*. London: Edward Arnold, 1984.

Lambarde, William. *A Perambulation of Kent*. London: Henry Middleton f. Ralph Newbury, 1576.

Lever, Thomas. *A fruitfull sermon made in Poules churche at London in the Shroudes the seconde daye of Februari 1550*. Edited by Edward Arber. English Reprints. London: E. Arber, 1870.

Lord, George deForest. *Homeric Renaissance: The Odyssey of George Chapman*. London: Macmillan, 1984.

Lopes de Mendoza, Iñigo, Marqués of Santillana. *The Prouberbes of the noble and woorthy souldier Sir Iames Lopez de Mendoza Marques of santillana, with the Paraphrase of D. Peter Diaz of Toldeo*. Translated by Barnabe Googe. London: R. Watkins, 1579.

Lydgate, John. *The Fall of Princes*. Edited by Henry Bergen. 4 vols. Washington, D.C.: Early English Text Society, 1924–27.

McKeown, Simon. "Barnabe Googe: Poetry and Society in the 1560s." Ph.D. diss., Queen's University of Belfast, 1993.

McKerrow, R. B., and R. S. Ferguson. *Title-Page Borders Used in England and Scotland, 1485–1640*. London: The Bibliographical Society, 1932.

Middleton, Richard. *Carde and Compasse of life*. London: W. S. f. Walter Burre, 1613.

Milton, John. *Paradise Lost*. Edited by Alastair Fowler. London: Longman, 1968.

Moon, John. *A History of Lamberhurst*. [England]: N.p., N.d.

Morland, William. *The Church in Lamberhurst*. 2nd ed. [England]: N.p., 1978.

Morris, John. *The Troubles of Our Catholic Forefathers*. 3 vols. London: N.p., 1872.

Muller, James Arthur. *Stephen Gardiner and the Tudor Reaction*. London: Society for Promoting Christian Knowledge, 1926.

Murrin, Michael. *The Veil of Allegory*. Chicago: University of Chicago Press, 1969.

Naogeorgus, Thomas. *The Popish Kingdome, or reigne of Antichrist.* Translated by Barnabe Googe. London: Henry Denham f. Richard Watkins, 1570.

Nixon, Anthony. *The Christian Navy.* London: Simon Stafford, 1602.

Odell, Thomas. *A brief and short Treatise. Called The Christians Pilgrimage to His Fatherland.* Amsterdam: John Fredericksz, 1635.

O'Sullivan, M. D. "Barnabe Googe: Provost Marshall of Connaught 1582–1585." *Journal of the Galway Archaeological and Historical Society* 18 (1938): 1–39.

Ovid. *Ovid's Fasti, with an English Translation by Sir James George Frazer.* Loeb Classical Library. New York: Putnam, 1931.

Owst, G. R. *Literature and the Pulpit in Medieval England.* 2nd ed. 1933. Oxford: Basil Blackwell, 1966.

P., A. *The Compasse of a Christian. Directing them that be tossed in the waues of this worlde vnto Christ Iesus.* London: J. Wolfe f. J. Harison the Younger, 1582.

Palingenius, Marcellus. *The Firste thre bokes . . . called the Zodyake of lyfe.* Translated by Barnabe Googe. London: John Tisdale f. Ralph Newbery, 1560.

——. *The Firste syxe bokes. . . .* Translated by Barnabe Googe. London: John Tisdale f. Ralph Newbery, 1561.

——. *The Zodiake of Life.* Translated by Barnabe Googe. London: Henry Denham f. Ralph Newbery, 1565.

——. *The Zodiake of Life, written by the excellent and Christian Poet, Marcellus Palingenius Stellatus (1576).* Translated by Barnabe Googe. Introduction by Rosemond Tuve. 1947. Delmar, N.J.: Scholars' Facsimiles and Reprints, 1976.

Palmer, Thomas. *The Emblems of Thomas Palmer: Two Hundred Poosees. Sloane MS 3794.* Edited by John Manning. AMS Studies in the Emblem 2. New York: AMS, 1988.

Peacham, Henry. *Minerva Britanna or a garden of heroical Devises.* London: Walter Dight, 1612.

Peirce, Brooke. "Barnabe Googe: Poet and Translator." Ph.D. diss., Harvard University, 1954.

Pickford, James. *The safegarde from ship-wracke or heaven's haven.* Douai: Peter Telv, 1618.

Pinkerton, William. "Barnabe Googe." *Notes and Queries* 3rd Ser. 3 (1863): 141–43, 181–84, 214–43, 301–2, 361–62.

Quarles, Francis. *Emblemes and Hieroglyphickes of the Life of Man (1638).* Introduction by Karl Josef Hoeltgen and John Horden. Emblematisches Cabinet. Hildesheim: Georg Olms, 1993.

Reusner, Nicolas. *Emblemata.* Frankfurt-am-Main: Johannes Feyerabendt, 1581.

Richardson, J. M. "Palingenius." *The Spenser Encyclopedia.* Edited by A. C. Hamilton et al. Toronto: University of Toronto Press, 1990, 1997. 526.

Ripa, Cesare. *Iconologia.* Translated by Pierce Tempest. London: Benjamin Motte, 1709.

Rogers, D. M., ed. *English Recusant Literature 1558–1640.* Vol. 9. Menston: Scolar, 1969.

Rufinus, Tyrannius, trans. *Ecclesiastica Historia diui Eusebii.* In *Ecclesiastica Historia diui Eusebii et Ecclesiastica historia gentis anglorum venerabilis Bede.* Strassburg: George Husner, 1500.

——, trans. *Eusebii ecclestica historia.* Edited by Theodore Mommsen. In Eusebius, edited by Schwartz.

St. Brandan, a Legend of the Sea. Edited by Thomas Wright. Percy Society. London: Percy Society, 1844.

Schleier, Reinhart. *Tabula Cebetis: oder Spiegel des Menschlichen Lebens.* Berlin: G. Mann, 1973.

Schuler, Robert M. "Three Renaissance Scientific Poems." *Studies in Philology* 75,5 (1978): 65–107.

Shakespeare, William. *The Complete Works.* Edited by Stanley Wells and Gary Taylor. Oxford: Oxford University Press, 1988.

——. *Hamlet.* Edited by Harold Jenkins. The Arden Shakespeare. London: Methuen, 1982.

——. *A Midsummer Night's Dream.* Edited by Harold F. Brooks. The Arden Shakespeare. London: Methuen, 1979.

——. *The Tempest.* Edited by Stephen Orgel. The Oxford Shakespeare. Oxford: Oxford University Press, 1987.

Sheidley, William E. *Barnabe Googe.* Boston: G. K. Hall, 1981.

Sidney, Philip. *The Countess of Pembroke's Arcadia.* Edited by Maurice Evans. London: Penguin, 1977.

Spenser, Edmund. *The Faerie Queene.* Edited by A. C. Hamilton. London: Longman, 1977.

——. *Poetical Works.* Edited by E. de Selincourt. Oxford: Oxford University Press, 1912.

——. *Selected Shorter Poems.* Edited by Douglas Brooks-Davies. London: Longman, 1995.

——. *The Yale Edition of the Shorter Poems of Edmund Spenser.* Edited by William A. Oram et al. New Haven: Yale University Press, 1989.

Stubbes, Phillip. *The Anatomie of Abuses.* London: Richard Jones, 1583.

Taylor, John (Water-Poet). *The Scvller Rowing From Tiber to Thames.* London, 1612.

Thomas, Keith. *Religion and the Decline of Magic: Studies in Popular Beliefs in Sixteenth- and Seventeenth-Century England.* 1971. London: Penguin, 1973.

Tilley, M. P. *A Dictionary of the Proverbs in England in the Sixteenth and Seventeenth Centuries.* Ann Arbor: University of Michigan Press, 1950.

Tuve, Rosemond. *Elizabethan and Metaphysical Imagery.* Chicago: University of Chicago Press, 1947.

——. *Allegorical Imagery: Some Medieval Books and Their Posterity.* Princeton: Princeton University Press, 1966.

Valeriano, Giovanni Piero. *Hieroglyphica.* Lyons: Paul Frellon, 1626.

Van der Noot, Jan. *A Theatre wherein be represented as wel the miseries & calamities that follow the voluptuous Worldlings, As also the greate ioyes and plesures which the faithfull do enioy.* London: Henry Bynneman, 1569.

Vergil. *The Aeneid of Vergil.* Translated by Kevin Guinagh. New York: Rinehart, 1953.

The Visitation of Kent. Harleian Soc. 75 (1924).

Warton, Thomas. *History of English Poetry.* Edited by W. Carew Hazlitt. 4 vols. London: Reeves and Turner, 1871.

Watson, Foster. *The English Grammar Schools to 1660: Their Curriculum and Practice.* Cambridge: Cambridge University Press, 1908.

——. *The* Zodiacus Vitae *of Marcellus Palingenius Stellatus: An Old School-Book.* London: Philip Wellsby, 1908.

Webbe, William. *A Discourse of English Poetrie (1586).* Edited by Edward Arber. English Reprints. London: E. Arber, 1870.

Weyer, Johann. *Witches, Devils, and Doctors in the Renaissance.* Edited by George Mora and Benjamin Kohl. Translated by John Shea. Binghamton, N.Y.: Medieval & Renaissance Texts & Studies, 1991. Translation of *De praestigiis daemonum* (1583).

Wharey, James Blanton. *A Study of the Sources of Bunyan's Allegories.* New York: Gordian Press, 1968.

Whitney, Geffrey. *A Choice of Emblemes and Other Devices.* Introduction by John Manning. Aldershot: Scolar, 1989.

Williams, Franklin B. *Index of Dedications and Commendatory Verses in English Books Before 1641.* London: The Bibliographic Society, 1962.

——. "An Initiation into Initials." *Studies in Bibliography* 9 (1957): 163–78.

——. "Renaissance Names in Masquerade." *PMLA* 69 (1954): 314–23.

Wilson, Dudley. *Signs and Portents: Monstrous Births from the Middle Ages to the Enlightenment.* London: Routledge, 1993.

Wither, George. *A Collection of Emblemes (1635).* Introduction by Michael Bath. Aldershot: Scolar, 1989.

GLOSSARY INDEX TO DEFINITIONS IN EXPLANATORY NOTES

The following words and expressions are defined in the Explanatory Notes for the line numbers given below. Unless otherwise indicated, the references are to the notes on "The Ship of safegarde."